THE
MANAGER'S
PROBLEM
SOLVER

THE
MANAGER'S
PROBLEM
SOLVER

Practical solutions to managers' questions

JOHN WALSH

Sphere Reference

Conceived, edited and designed by
Marshall Editions Ltd.
170 Piccadilly, London
W1V 9DD

TRADE
MARK

SPHERE

Editor:
Erica Hunningher
Art Editor:
George Glaze
Assistant Editor:
Louise Tucker
Design Assistants:
Kim Coppard
Simon Wilson
Financial Consultant:
Paul Thimont, BA, FCA
Managing Editor:
Ruth Binney
Production: Janice Storr

First published 1987 by
Sphere Books Ltd.
27 Wrights Lane
London W8 5TZ
Copyright © 1987
Marshall Editions Ltd.

Filmset in Century Schoolbook by
Vision Typesetting, Manchester, UK
Origination by
Alpha Reprographics, Harefield, UK
Printed and bound by
Usines Brepols SA, Belgium

John Walsh, MA, a
journalist specializing
in management, has
talked to hundreds of
managers all over the
world. His understanding
of real management
issues enables him to
offer fresh and practical
solutions to the many
problems encountered
by the managers of today.

He was educated at the
universities of Oxford
and Dublin. He has been
Associate and Publications
Editor of *The Director* and
contributes to a wide
range of newspapers
and magazines.

The author would like to
thank the following for
their invaluable
contribution to problem
solving:
George Bull,
management writer.
David Harvey, Editor of
*Business Computing
and Communications.*
Carolyn Hart,
journalist and
businesswoman.

CONTENTS

INTRODUCTION

Management means getting things done. It conjures decisions out of a fog of possibilities, initiates action and selects people to carry it out. It makes things happen, whether it be the purchase of a copying machine, the acquisition of a company or the chairing of a steering committee on nuclear waste. As a result, management tends to give itself airs, as though it dealt only in foolproof systems and efficient structures. This, as any business executive knows, is a long way from the truth.

For the average manager of a department, a workshop, a production line, a service sector, a platoon, a research unit or a car-spares shop, far more time is devoted during the ordinary working day to 'fire-fighting' tiny problems, reversals and procedural hiccups than in overseeing the smooth passage of work. The problems of colleagues, delegatees and bosses must be given a hearing. Time must be fitted in for paperwork, forward planning and budgeting.

Technological innovations, at least, must be understood. Mistakes must be rectified. Late deliveries, debts or servicing must be countered. And some time must be allowed for seeing to one's own health, welfare, domestic stability, personal growth and career progress. These are the myriad problems that accompany the running of any organization. They need solutions that are practical, useful, simple and effective.

This book seeks to offer the manager just such practical help, by identifying the most likely problems he or she faces and offering answers to them. It is not a manual of management theory. It espouses no single system or philosophy. It accepts that there are some problems to which no solutions can be found. It draws on several sources of business wisdom: the pronouncements of transatlantic management writers; pieces of advice gleaned from experienced businessmen around the world; specific answers to questions from consultants in specific fields, from finance to feminism; and several random incidents of lateral thinking and straight talking from colleagues and friends.

The resulting 250-odd questions and answers have the comforting style of magazine problem pages; which serves to emphasize that management deals more closely with life than with theories of work throughput. It is as much a learnable art as the other Humanities. And its central skill is that least academic of virtues: common sense.

John Walsh.

Q

I have an MA in Business Studies and am looking for a job. Many of the management advertisements ask for specific character traits and strengths, but I'm not in the habit of constant self-analysis. So how do I find out what I might be good at?

There are many areas of everyday experience in which your fundamental skills reveal themselves. Each temperamental trait has an analogue in business life. Try to identify them, and relate them to work.

Physical skills
● Are you attracted to physical activities that depend on rhythm and energy (dancing, golf, swimming)? You're probably disposed to organized and methodical work.
● Are you keen on sports that demand coordination and instant reactions (tennis, squash, judo, football)? You're instinctive, combative and reactive, performing best when the adrenalin is flowing and problems are flying at you.
● Do you enjoy combining dexterity with creativity (crafts, drawing, gardening)? Your skills might be useful in project development.

Intellectual skills
● Do you enjoy puzzles, conundrums and crosswords? Their combination of free association and lateral thinking mark you down as a clear thinker and problem-solver.
● Can you work through ideas in your head while, for instance, looking out of a train window? You don't yield to distractions and would suit a position that called for protracted periods of concentration.
● Do you always need hard information in front of you before you can make a decision? You should be in the finance department, or be the office manager.

Technical skills
● Do you fiddle with engines, cars, old radios and persevere until they are fixed? If so, you may be a natural engineer, but more importantly you're someone who believes a solution exists somewhere – a valuable person to be in charge of a special project.
● Do you follow instructions step-by-step or do you race ahead? You're not a natural subject for advanced training if the latter's the case.
● Does a job get done when you promise yourself you'll do it or when you're talked into it? Are you a natural supervisor, or an efficient, if stubborn, supervisee?

Interpersonal skills
● Are you a good talker, an anecdotalist, a master of repartee? Depending on which you are, you might be a marketeer, a whizz in meetings or an extrovert team leader.
● Do people tell you their problems and try to enlist your support? If so, you might become a sympathetic leader.
● Do you get your own way when two of you are deciding where to eat? How about when six of you are deciding? This might indicate how forceful or conciliatory you are. If you always impose your ideas, avoid commitees – their lengthy procedures will frustrate you.

Q

Although I've a good, logical mind and a flair for organization, I'm rather uncreative and tend to lose my temper with people who don't follow my instructions precisely. What can I do about these failings?

Try to disguise or detract from your weaknesses at all times. You must minimize the negative traits in your character if you want to influence the majority of your staff.

Enlist the help of trusted colleagues. One should be intuitive, with long-term notions of where the company is heading. The other should be a diplomat: an extrovert, able to talk as easily to the chief executive as to the receptionist, happy to explain things more than once.

Listen to your creative colleague's ideas and match them with your common sense to see if a workable synthesis is possible.

Use your diplomat tactfully, and only now and again, to interpret your instructions to a team on your behalf.

Q

I am constantly accused of having an 'unbusinesslike' approach, of being too subjective, even though my value judgments are often correct. Should I ignore my instincts at work?

No, you should always be aware of your own emotions and how they colour issues. Your passionate nature can easily confuse its own sincerity for the rightness of the issue under discussion. It is better to reach a decision by logic, testing, double-checking and research.

In 1953 Professor Chris Argyris, the American industrial relations writer, surveyed the characteristics that help an executive thrive. They included:

● A high tolerance of frustration.

● A liking for meetings in which ideas can be freely examined.

● A constant, critical self-questioning.

'These executives', he wrote, 'were keenly aware that their personal biases, their personal ways of seeing the world, were not necessarily the only or the best ways . . . They respected their own judgment, not as always being correct, but as always being made with the best possible intentions.'

Q

I like my work and I'm good at it. But I don't fit in with most of the people who reach the top in my firm. Why can't I be one of them?

The only way out of this psychological conundrum is to identify the reason for your isolation and try to overcome it.

Think about what the job entails, what you're good at, what you're contributing to the company and who stands above and below you in the hierarchy. Then consider the profiles of the people who get to the top. Remind yourself where you all stand in company terms.

Once you've clarified your business relationships, it should be easier to regard the others as true colleagues. You're all employed by the same organization, to pursue the same ends of profit and job satisfaction, and the sooner you conquer your feelings of being different the better.

Q

What causes stress?

It is important to recognize the potential stress that goes with any responsible job.

Successfully met, the challenge is both stimulating and satisfying. But when the pressure becomes too great, the challenge too hard to meet and the responsibility too great to bear, it is all too easy to get swept into the stress spiral.

When stress sets in, it becomes impossible to regain your equilibrium – to calm down, relax and sleep soundly, even to eat properly.

Work is badly affected and home ceases to be a haven, which leads the harassed manager into yet more stressful territory.

Change
Job mismatch
Role ambiguity
Overwork
Underwork/boredom
Failure
Success
Deteriorating
relationships

Increased or decreased
responsibility
Isolation
Lack of exercise/hobbies
Ill health

Feel bad tempered	Feel suspicious
Feel like crying	Can't remember things
Can't concentrate	Dread the future
Can't make decisions	Depressed

Tiredness	Raised blood pressure
Headaches	Skin eruptions
Thudding heart	Trembling
Indigestion	Breathlessness

Mind racing
Feel guilty
Feel inadequate
Crave alcohol

Dependence on
cigarettes

Cramps
Muscle spasms
Insomnia
Frequent hangovers

Loss of appetite
Shakiness
Loss of libido

Q

I know I'm under stress and can recognize all the obvious symptoms. Is this the time for a complete change of direction in my life?

You may well need a radical change of lifestyle at home and at work. Approach the problem by drawing up a plan of campaign. Your well-being must take precedence.

First, visit the doctor and arrange for a full health screen. This should include:

1 A full personal history, including details of your smoking and drinking habits.
2 Height and weight: to assess any obesity.
3 Lung function test and chest X-ray.
4 Blood pressure measurement.
5 ECG (electro-cardiograph): to analyze the heartbeat when resting and exercising.
6 Urine and blood tests: to assess, for example, liver function.

There is much you can do to help yourself out of the vicious spiral of stress. For instance:
● Get enough sleep. Ascertain how many hours you need each night and make sure you get them, even if you have to take sleeping tablets as a stop-gap.
● Clear the trivia from your working life. If you feel a nagging guilt about letters you've not got round to writing, do them all one morning, before starting the day's work.

● Learn to say no. When trivia encroach, simply respond with 'Sorry, I can't . . . up to my eyes.'
● Get control of your time with a time system diary.
● Rethink your career and which of your daily activities truly contribute to it or move you closer to your goal. If you decide you're in the wrong job, work out what you *do* want – and how you'll achieve it. Then go for it.
● Assess how much your home and family mean to you. Work out what you would do, who you would see, if you had three months to live. Start doing and seeing *now*.
● Look ahead. See what can be done about the less pleasant parts of a job that is generally congenial.
● Consider a change of job within the company.
● Stop feeling isolated. Make a firm undertaking to get to know your staff better.
● Rethink your social life. Over the next six months, give six Sunday lunch parties (no close colleagues allowed).
● Take more exercise. Ask a friend to jog/play tennis with you.
● Tell yourself you're in charge of your life again.

Do these and you won't become the next victim of killer stress.

Q

Conflicting priorities often make me feel stressed. How can I resolve them?

Stress reflects a failure to operate from a base of inner certainty and self-esteem. You ought to be aware of your rights as an individual whose emotional and physical needs exist independently of your work role.

Believe in your rights:
● To be treated with respect as a capable and equal human being.
● To state your personal needs and set your own priorities.
● To express your feelings, opinions and values.
● To say yes and no for yourself.
● To make mistakes.
● To ask for what you want.
● To decline responsibility for other people's problems.
● To deal with other people without being dependent on them for approval.

Believe in your rights and act on them with conviction. You'll be better equipped to prevent personal stress.

Q

Do business people suffer from stress more than other members of the community?

Not necessarily. It can be just as stressful to be at home with a group of demanding children. However, it is certainly true that modern business life is fraught with conditions tailor-made to cause stress.

In business, the following are among the most potent:
● Urgent, must-get-there-on-time travel.
● Financial worries.
● Fear of redundancy.
● Fear of failure.
● Lack of confidence.
● Noisy working conditions.
● Constant effort to impress.
● Regular confrontations with subordinates.
● Endless flood of details for checking or approval.
● Constant decision making.
● Pressure from a spouse to achieve/earn more.
● Fear of a wrong career direction and thus of a wasted life.

Above all, because business employees tend to see work achievement as indicative of success in life generally, they are more likely to respond to minor irritants and reversals as though they were major disasters, with the inevitable stress-provoking reactions.

Q

I think of myself as a competent manager but am hounded by thoughts of failure, dismissal and disaster. I know this is unreasonable, but how do I stop?

The fear of failure is an inevitable response to the relentless pursuit of achievement. Every manager is naturally anxious to do well – and the assumption is that success comes from never doing anything wrong.

The truth is, of course, that everyone who makes decisions makes a bad one from time to time. It's a phenomenon of our culture that we've made failure a bogeyman. We get caught up in the demoralizing circle of failing/worrying/losing confidence/failing.

Try a new approach to problem solving:
1 Tackle each problem realistically. Don't assume there's a single perfect solution – there rarely is. Try to work out your chances of success dispassionately and see if they can be improved.
2 Assess the importance of each situation from different perspectives.
3 Admit you were wrong. Make known the extent of the mishap and how you plan to counter it.
4 Don't blame others, or your own disposition to failure. Find out why you went wrong and learn from your mistake.

Q

I'm a fighter and a survivor, and stress doesn't bother me. Should I worry that I don't worry?

Everybody needs a certain amount of stress if they're to perform at the top of their potential. You're obviously the 'test pilot type' who never loses the thrill of taking risks with the unknown and who enjoys constant challenge and excitement.

But even test pilots have days off, so don't be tempted to take on so much that you risk burn-out. However little you feel the need, make sure you regularly:
● Take a holiday (at least once a year).
● Day dream.
● Exercise.
● Spend time with friends and family.
● Talk about subjects other than work.
● Read books not connected with work.
● Remind yourself that life starts rather than stops at 5.30.

Conflict and crisis **88–9** *Working conditions* **98–9**

Q

I travel to America and the Far East a few times a year. I've never found a cure for jetlag, and don't quite understand it. What's the best remedy?

Jetlag affects almost everyone who flies, in ways they often don't even realize.

An experiment conducted by British businessman David Moreau in collaboration with NASA and TWA established that almost every body-system was disturbed by changes in time zones:

● Manual dexterity is impaired.
● Soundness of judgment decreases by 20 per cent.
● Reflexes are dulled.

People also become more volatile (especially if confronted by slight aggression soon after arrival), insomniac, forgetful, depressed to the point of paranoia, clumsy and susceptible to colds.

Adjusting to a new time scale itself takes time. Some sources suggest you need a full day's relaxation for every hour lost or gained.

In the absence of any effective remedy, all you can do is to minimize the risk of damage:

1 Choose the most sensible flights. Ideally you should reach your destination in the early evening, in time for a shower, dinner and an early night. Try to do without sleeping pills.
2 Plan ahead. It helps to prepare for your destination by going to bed and getting up an hour earlier than usual, and adjusting your meal times to a new 'body clock' rhythm.
3 Don't fight to stay awake on the plane. Seven hours' sleep per day (however distributed) is a necessity for the average traveller.
4 It is not necessary to deny yourself alcohol completely, but go easy – one drink too many will worsen your jetlag.
5 Adjust yourself mentally to the time scale at your destination as soon as possible. Set your watch to the new time and think to yourself, 'Ah, it'll be lunchtime soon', even though your internal system is shouting that it's really 3 am. When you arrive, don't spend the first day reminding yourself of the time back home. There is, however, one exception to this rule:
6 Don't take important decisions at times when you would normally be asleep. Travel, shifted time zones, and food at the 'wrong' time will have reduced your judgment. Delay making any business decisions until after your first proper night's sleep.

Q

On long plane journeys I find myself fretting about the possibility of losing my luggage, about the reception at the other end and whether I'm wasting valuable time just getting from A to B. Is this usual?

Certainly. It's difficult to relax on a plane, however hard the cabin crew tries to help. The way to minimize worry is shrewd planning.

You should never have to be concerned about money and documents: keep your wallet, credit card case, chequebook, travellers' cheques, passport and air ticket close at hand at all times. To obviate the possibility of losing your luggage, take it on the plane with you. Choose a flat leather portfolio travel case or a bulky holdall that conforms to the airlines' requirements regarding hand baggage.

Doing some in-flight work is good for you. Anything that makes you feel more assured and prepared for the meetings at your destination will increase your sense of well-being.

The main reason for doing some work is to make you relaxed and drowsy. After an hour's concentration, have a snooze or bury yourself in the latest Jeffrey Archer.

Q

I've been offered an excellent job in a company 150 miles away from my home. Door to door, the journey to work would be a little under three hours. Should I go for a lesser job nearer home?

A third of your life is spent asleep and a third at work, so it seems unduly hard on yourself to squander so much on travelling. Consider the stress on your personal life.
● When will you take exercise/relax?
● What about your social life?

Most at stake is your home life:
● If you have a permanent relationship, how does your partner feel about your late return home?
● If you have children, how are you going to play a part in their lives?

You will be an unsatisfactory partner and parent. Your family will rebel, and so, after a while, will you.

If the job is spectacularly lucrative, you might treat it like an oil-rig contract and endure the journey for a while or rent a room near your work and go home for weekends.

But, unless you're single, and keen on reading novels for long periods, go for a job nearer home.

Q

I commute from the suburbs into the city every day, surrounded by readers of newspapers and books, wool-gatherers and chatterers. Doesn't anyone believe in using their transit time to get some valuable work done?

Your fellow travellers on train and tube aren't wasting their travel time. They're sensibly using it to relax before embarking on the choppy waves of office life.

How much would really be gained by working on agenda or drafted reports for the 40-odd minutes at your disposal?

You're not duty bound to work all the time. You're certainly not being paid to do so. Far better that you should use the time for enjoyment and preparation:
1 Try some deep breathing exercises.
2 Stretch your limbs, in sequence, starting with your fingers and ending with your shoulder blades, as though giving yourself a massage.
3 Close your eyes and think of the next occasion to look forward to: the barbecue on Saturday, your daughter's birthday next week.

You should arrive at work a happier person than you set out.

Q

I've been given a new company car and, although it handles superbly, I'm surprised to find myself getting to work just as bad tempered as when I drove my old one. Where's the flaw?

You're just one of millions of travel stress victims, people who are badly affected by getting from A to B, whether they're driving a Rolls or a tricycle.

No one knows why well-balanced people change personalities once inside a car. It's been attributed to claustrophobia, to a sense of being 'untouchable', and to the release of individual 'power' impulses that bring out the Mussolini in the mildest executive.

Remember how that car in the rear-view mirror this morning seemed to be following you? The woman who got closer and closer behind until you swore at her?

These feelings are symptoms of travel stress:
● Your sense of rules, of correctness and transgression, become all-important.
● Your inner hostility and fear of others come to the surface.

Unfortunately, travel stress is a fact of life and does not lend itself to a solution. Unless you go for the supremely obvious one: get a chauffeur.

Q

My husband and I are at daggers drawn. I have been promoted to a senior position in another city. I want to go. I've explained to him about relocation allowances and have found schools for the children, but he's determined to stay, even though he could easily find work in the new city. How can I change his mind?

Only by logic. The importance of your new challenge clearly outweighs other considerations for you – but the wishes of your whole family must be taken into account.

To persuade him, you might draw attention to:
● Your salary after promotion, which should be a telling indication of how highly you're regarded professionally.
● Your relocation allowance and housing expenses, which will probably mean being able to afford a better home than your present one.
● Your disruption bonus, removals bonus or displacement factor.
● The additional allowances (car, clothes, entertainment) you'll be given as head of a provincial division.
● The great step forward it will give your career.
● The opportunity to make a fresh start in a new town.

Against this he may argue that:
● His work contacts will be lost by a move to a new city.
● His friends, sporting partners and other acquaintances will be left behind, as well as the friends you've made jointly over the years.
● The children must abandon their playmates and start as outsiders in new schools.
● He will have to forgo (1) his Tuesday night woodwork class (2) his climbing roses (3) his trips to the secondhand bookshop.

You will counter, quite fairly, with the argument that your salary is more substantial and therefore more important.

You will point out that woodwork, roses and old books are available anywhere.

You will insist that the children will regard the move as an adventure and so should he.

In the end it will be a straight battle between money and power on one side and domesticity and *status quo* on the other. If he's not the sort of spouse to respond to the attractions of Mammon then your last resort is to say that, since this is potentially the most important step of your life, you must take it or you will never forgive yourself.

Perhaps that will encourage him to help you take the plunge.

Q

I've recently been elevated from secretarial to managerial status. I'm anxious to shine in a hitherto all-male hierarchy, but it means working late and sometimes bringing papers home. This makes my husband irritated – how do I balance the two halves of my life?

Your desire to shine may be making you try too hard. Why jeopardize your marriage just to show you're better than your male colleagues?

The fact that you've successfully breached a masculine preserve means that you've already won that battle.

Try to relax in your new job and stamp your own style on it, rather than feel you must be outstanding. Don't spend longer at work after 5.30pm than is necessary to straighten out your workload for the next day.

That said, your husband's attitude seems unreasonable. Now you're becoming an executive he needs to adjust, too. Maybe he's jealous of your status, or feels threatened by your competitiveness.

Getting the balance right demands tact and firmness. You must accord home and work equal weight.

Q

My wife complains that she never sees me, and my children are virtual strangers. Yet my job is important for the family's financial security. How can I review my priorities?

If the family's financial security is important, why is their emotional security less so? Neglect your family in favour of the spurious importance of the office, its hierarchy and politics, and you may find you haven't got a family with which to enjoy the future.

Obviously you are aware of this already. You're trapped in an invidious position:
● Your wife says that you never take her out. You argue back that without your hard work and long hours the mortgage would never get paid and you would be living like gypsies.
● She says that gypsies probably have a much better time than your family, and at least the fathers know what their children look like.
● You retort that if this ingratitude is all you slave away for you might as well stop now . . .

But you can't stop working. You must make money to provide for the family's needs. What you may be failing to remember is that they, and not the job, represent the bottom line – the final justification for what you do. The job is the means, they are the end. If, by your working habits, you prejudice their happiness,

or even the future of the family as a unit, then you are actively countering what you first set out to do.

So what is the answer? First, resolve to reduce your working hours, and make this possible by delegating more, organizing your time more effectively and learning to say no.

Second, plan some family weekends – in the garden or the park, redecorating the house, visiting friends, having drinks, dinner or lunch parties, going on outings to the country. In all these, include the family in your newly time-managed life.

Third, take your wife out at least one evening a week, or do something together that's nothing to do with work. Why not take up a sport or hobby you can share, or replan the design of the house or garden together?

Fourth, reacquaint yourself with your children. Join in their activities – or simply play with them. It will be as much fun for you as for them. Start going to school functions. No job should make you miss seeing them in the school play or swimming gala.

Q

I've been offered a major-league posting overseas. The money's excellent (and tax free) but the contract is for two years and would involve the whole family in upheaval. What kind of relocation package should I be seeking?

However big the financial rewards, you must first consider whether you're really suited to the expatriate life. You need vast reserves of patience, resilience, self-confidence and adaptability. Equally, the working life far from your roots is no place for the introvert or recluse.

Financially, the usual remuneration-plus-benefits package is home salary plus:
● Overseas allowance, paid in local currency and linked to the local cost of living.
● Company house.
● Furnishing allowance.
● All travel costs.
● Local entertainment allowance.
● Car.
● Health insurance.

Companies generally also pay 100 per cent of school costs, even if you decide that boarding school at home is the best option.

In case of emergencies, the family is also supplied with free return tickets home at least once a year.

You should expect six weeks' leave a year.

MANAGING YOURSELF / JOB PROFILES

Q

Is it possible to generalize about 'good managers'? Surely every management job is different, and demands different skills and responsibilities?

There is, of course, a great deal of difference between a hotel's Personnel manager, a steel foundry's supply manager and a retail chain's area sales manager. But all three, however diverse their businesses and precise their job descriptions, have to perform common functions. Their jobs demand:

● Well thought out action plans and organizational procedures.

● Concern with the long-term goals of the business, balancing personal ambition and the reaching of individual targets with these wider considerations.

● Imaginative and effective delegation of tasks to subordinates who will carry them out efficiently.

● Leadership by example.

● Strong motivation of those whom they command.

● Constant measurement of performance, to determine whether a more effective working method might be used.

● Constant advancement of the functions and effectiveness of a department.

● The ability to deal simultaneously with scores of everyday problems and reversals.

● The drawing together of the various departmental strands of an operation.

The sales team, the hotel Personnel staff and the heavy industry boffins are all variations on a theme. They are the departmental staff whose function is to be used by the manager to achieve the most effective possible deployment of resources and labour:

● The job done as required.

● High standards achieved and maintained.

● Work done in the shortest possible time, or to meet a predetermined deadline with no loss of quality.

● Work done as inexpensively as possible, or within a given budget.

Q

So many advertised jobs reveal little besides a title, a salary and a description of the department. How can I sort out the most promising jobs?

Advertisements cannot answer all your questions. Apply for jobs that attract your attention, but before accepting any of them, establish, during or after the interview:

1 The company's reputation. It may seem premature to consider the firm's name, but it will reflect on you.

2 The department in which you will be working. Is it large, friendly, hierarchical or multi-disciplinary?

3 The track record of the management team in the department you may join.

4 The exact nature of your duties.

5 The degree of liaison between departments.

6 The chain of command – your immediate boss and his respective superior. The extent of your likely authority.

7 The total remuneration package. Check if it includes (a) private health insurance; (b) company car; (c) company credit cards, travel and entertainment allowance.

Teams and groups **62–5** *Scheduling* **66–7** *Delegation* **68–9**

The staff I'm responsible for seem to care more about their job titles than the quality of their work. Should I dispense with titles altogether?

Business titles should never be underestimated as motivational tools. Employees who sneer at business hierarchies tend to bury their cynicism when they're upgraded from 'Junior' to 'Senior' assistant.

That said, ever since the men who washed the windows on the Empire State Building were named 'Transparent Wall Cleansing Operatives' we have ceased to trust business titles.

The answer is to keep a sense of balance. If necessary, give everyone on a similar level the title of Associate or Vice President to indicate that they are medium-range operators.

Avoid the use of meaningless titles that merely mask inefficiency. No one should feel that their title makes them unsackable.

How can I determine the tasks for which I am personally responsible?

As a manager, you are responsible for scrutinizing the demands made on you by the organization:
● What work is required?
● By when?
● Following which procedures?

You must then redefine the tasks in the context of your staff resources.

What you're essentially responsible for, therefore, is the macro-scale coordination of large projects, which you cut up into manageable portions by judicious delegation.

At the end of the project, or by the deadline imposed from above, you'll be held responsible for whatever results.

Take a look at your job description, specifically at the 'responsibilities' section. You'll find that most of your time is supposed to be spent in allocating work, checking it, motivating those who work for you and coordinating their activities.

There should be very few tasks as finite, individual acts which you are personally expected to carry out.

A new chief executive has taken over our company and has installed a trainee in the sales department, where I am assistant manager. The trainee has begun to take over my work as invoicing supervisor. What can I do?

Check your job description or ask Personnel to confirm the nature of your duties.

If any of the tasks, activities, duties or responsibilities that are supposed to be yours have been taken over by another, with the connivance of the chief executive, your status and future are at risk.

But don't panic. Enter a formal complaint to your immediate superior stating that your efficiency is threatened. Say that you are being prevented from doing your duties because of the interloper.

If your boss fails to reestablish your position, seek legal advice. You might have a case for charging the company with 'constructive dismisssal'.

Q

I've been asked by the board to provide a description of my job 'for appraisal and review'. This sounds ominous. How do I write it to maximum effect?

Being asked to provide your bosses with a job description is nothing to worry about. The purpose of an appraisal is to improve understanding between managers.

Describing your job helps you to define:
● The demands made on you.
● The demands you make on people and resources.
● The decisions for which you are responsible.
● The boundaries within which you operate.

Describing your job should make you consider:
● What would happen if the job ceased to exist?
● How your responsibilities differ from those of your colleagues and superiors.
● At what point in your decision making must you defer to the authority of others?
● How your boss checks your work: by the lack of problems or complaints, by reporting back or by positive reinforcement?

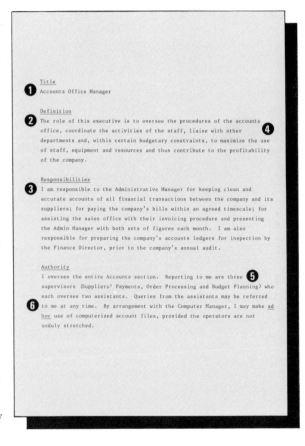

Title
Accounts Office Manager

Definition
The role of this executive is to oversee the procedures of the accounts office, coordinate the activities of the staff, liaise with other departments and, within certain budgetary constraints, to maximize the use of staff, equipment and resources and thus contribute to the profitability of the company.

Responsibilities
I am responsible to the Administrative Manager for keeping clean and accurate accounts of all financial transactions between the company and its suppliers; for paying the company's bills within an agreed timescale; for assisting the sales office with their invoicing procedure and presenting the Admin Manager with both sets of figures each month. I am also responsible for preparing the company's accounts ledgers for inspection by the Finance Director, prior to the company's annual audit.

Authority
I oversee the entire Accounts section. Reporting to me are three supervisors (Suppliers' Payments, Order Processing and Budget Planning) who each oversee two assistants. Queries from the assistants may be referred to me at any time. By arrangement with the Computer Manager, I may make ad hoc use of computerized account files, provided the operators are not unduly stretched.

1 Specify full title and department.

2 Keep the definition formal and precise. Describe what you're there for, not what you do.

3 What do you do in the ordinary working day/week? In this section specify the executive at whom your work is aimed, and exactly what happens along the way. Itemize a few tasks, if not necessarily all, but write in detail what you're expected to provide at the end of the chain.

4 Liaison is a handy word, implying sharp-end communication with other departments. It should be used sparingly to indicate your peer group or parallel department.

5 Identify the echelons which serve you with reports, items for checking, and down-stream manual or shopfloor activities.

❶ Title
Assistant Production Manager, ceramic tiles division

❷ Definition
The role of this executive is to assist the Production Manager in the smooth running of the manufacturing process in plants 3,4,5 and 6; to oversee the arrival of relevant materials and the delivery of finished goods to distribution outlets for retail sale, and thus contribute to the profitability of the company.

Responsibilities
❸ In a normal week, my function is to liaise with the suppliers of powdered clay from the Norfolk quarries, determine the amount required above or below standard quota, and present figures to the Production Manager for
❹ approval. Then to liaise with the plant supervisors concerning personnel or time scale difficulties, and duly report to the Manager. To receive reports from glazing works as to the maintenance and working order of machinery. To supervise quality control between stages of baking clay and glazing tile. To oversee stacking, warehousing, packing and freight on to distributing lorries.

Authority
I have supervisory power over most of the manufacturing process, and am authorized to abort the process in an emergency. Suppliers, plant supervisors, glazing workers, quality checkers and storage operatives
❺ report to me. I report to the Production Manager, who has overall power to increase or decrease, start or stop, improve or maintain, any aspect of production work. Sometimes I'm asked to report direct to the Managing **❻** Director, for example over local technical difficulties or labour relations problems.

6 This section should be precise about your powers of veto and initiative. Who exactly reports to you? Have you a direct line to the boardroom?

Q

Now I'm a manager, I never seem to do the jobs I'm good at and which earned me the promotion. Is this inevitable?

It's inevitable that you should stop carrying out tasks yourself and start getting other people to do them for you.

It's not inevitable that you should feel a sense of loss – indeed, the best new managers are happy to be released from job-drudgery and able, at last, to put others to work.

It sounds as though you're a do-er in an organizer's role, unwilling to give up the satisfying once-a-week tasks of counting the paper clips and filing the remittance slips.

You're too grown up now to be pining for a security blanket. Managers exist to organize, plan, mobilize, motivate and initiate effective action. Start getting side-tracked into quotidian little jobs, and your planning or monitoring will show gaps.

Think projects, not details. Think big. Forget the paper clips.

Q

I've been in the same company for ten years. It's successful but doesn't seem to have changed at all in that time. Should I move on?

Why on earth should you? If the company is making a steady profit, the surroundings and personnel are congenial and the future looks untroubled and rosy, why are you complaining?

If your own work gets done without undue feelings of boredom or frustration and, above all, if you don't feel the need for a change, for Heaven's sake stay put and count your blessings.

Change doesn't always mean success. If your company is successful, and consistently so, it's probably for a very simple reason: it has the sense to stick to what it's good at.

Q

The outgoing manager of my new department worked there for 10 years, and I get the impression that everyone expects me to stick to the same work routines. What can I do?

Ignore them. You have to find your own rhythm and your own working level. That means establishing a set of procedures that suits you:
● Clear your desk of paraphernalia. Discard all memos. Keep the letters and filed documents from the last six months only.
● Tell your secretary the times of day at which you prefer to (a) sign letters, (b) receive visitors, (c) discuss problems or appointments.
● Dictate or hand-write all your letters by the same time each day (say a deadline of 4.30).
● Have your name written on all files as well as on the door.

If colleagues persist in extolling the virtues of your predecessor's system, try this trick. Before you throw out most of the old papers, look through the Special Project Files and find those relating to unfinished projects. Analyze how much their failure was due to the previous incumbent's systems management.

Then make your conclusions known.

Q

I see a mountain of papers heading my way from all corners of the department. I don't know yet which data will be relevant. Can I find out instantly, or should I read every word of every page?

Don't let a tidal wave of paper engulf you.

Demand to see only what is relevant to the work you're managing. Break the paper down into sections so that the most important or significant figures will always be close to hand. The separate areas of information vary widely from company to company, but the following 'reading pile' (from Iaconetti and O'Hara's *First Time Manager*) offers a fairly comprehensive selection:

● Production reports.
● Sales reports.
● Customer/client/ patient statistics.
● Complaint reports.
● Error reports.
● Audit reports.
● Work schedules.
● Payroll sheets.
● Job descriptions.
● Work flow charts/Unit organization charts.

The authors suggest that you should raid your secretary's desk, and the filing system itself, in search of reports under these headings. Then contact the individual sections, asking for any information relating to your department.

Q

I've recently been promoted. There's one member of staff who won't acknowledge this and refuses to allow me to check her work, for which I am responsible. What can I do?

Resentments often break out when one member of a peer group rises above the others. Think of it from her point of view – how would you like it if you were called upon to defer to a colleague?

You've got to act the part or you'll never be taken seriously.

Make a fuss of the new office space available to you. Get new cards and stationery printed. Arrange to see all your immediate subordinates one-to-one.

You are responsible for the work which emanates from the department. So you'll have to pull rank. Explain that, while you're still the same people, you now stand at a slightly different professional angle to one another. You must now oversee and supervise, while she continues to make her valuable contribution. That's all that has changed.

If this fails, appeal to her good sense: if there's a discrepancy in the department's output, would she be happy for the board to hear that it was mutiny? Does she want to risk her job due to personal rivalry?

Q

My company has been bought out by a conglomerate, and my department is to merge with several others. Is this the end of the line for my job, or a new beginning?

Conglomerates are usually better disposed toward the financial than the personal assets of new acquisitions. Whatever section or department you're running, they will already have one; so either they will combine the two or, more likely, leave your section to run as before, but reporting to a new boss.

The senior managers of companies larger or richer than one's own are rarely shy of showing their feelings about managerial incompetence, and tension-building rows will inevitably punctuate the first few weeks of the new regime. Old ways of managing departmental processes will encounter new ways of managing the company overall.

Think of your future career. Before the takeover your route to the top could be kept in sight. Now you are surrounded by new concentric circles of management, and the peaks and troughs of the hierarchy have become obscured. It will now take you exactly twice as long as before to get to the top.

Q

Who holds the final decision-making power in a company?

In every company, power is wielded at senior management level, by the board of voting directors, under the guidance of the chairman. Top executive power is shared between the managing and finance directors, and is then dispersed through the various departments in a series of balanced commitments.

For example, a sales director unconcerned about a production director's needs will have no influence over quality and output levels. A marketing director must convince the MD of the efficacy of a proposed strategy before market research finance will be forthcoming.

The strategies of the ambitious are responsible for much intra-company power broking, especially during times of change. A wise manager is constantly aware of what the future may hold and acts accordingly.

In companies whose board members own substantial shareholdings, or who meet the family owners socially, dozens of small alliances may be forged, threatened or broken, in order to head off unpopular decisions or to restrain the ambitions of the powerful.

Q

The managing director of my company seems no more than a figurehead. Somebody else must be taking the big decisions. How can I find out who it is?

It's probable that in fact it is the managing director who's taking the decisions, or at least being seen to do so. The question really is, who's influencing him the most?

Power and influence are distinct but interrelated managerial concepts. Having power to get your own way – by bullying or by veto – is one thing. Wielding influence without leaving fingerprints is another.

The most influential people in a business are often far from obvious. They are practised in the arts of the corridor discussion, the pre-meeting meeting, the whispered aside, the unofficial briefing. They are adept at netting and evaluating every new idea that swims into the company, and delivering a polished reaction to the MD before anyone else has the chance.

They'll present themselves, too, as the boss's most devoted officers in dealing with the fault-finding board.

Detecting levels of influence is virtually impossible, but the executive secretary to the MD is certainly someone worth cultivating.

Q

Apart from arbitrary considerations, such as company rank, where do company bosses get their power?

● Money. Having control of the most flexible and potent of all resources means that they can alter the entire direction of the company – and thus of all its personnel – if they so wish.
● Knowledge. Understanding markets, receiving inside information about company movements, appreciating the businesses that are likely to boom in the future and controlling the flow of information to manipulate people and decisions. You can never know too much.
● Contacts. Being in touch with other powerful people means that vast projects can be discussed – and zillion-dollar agreements ratified – at the sports club, over lunch or in the bar.
● Labour. The power to hire and fire, to elevate and cast down, to establish or sabotage careers, gives the bosses a kind of omnipotence in the labour market.
● Loyalty. Bosses who do well by their staff, making them feel fulfilled and proud in furthering their leader's interests have unseen and unquantifiable power. No money can match that.

Q

At my interview I was assured that the company was 'one big happy family'. A month into the job, the company shows signs of being divided. How could I have found this out in advance?

It's far from easy to find out more than the hard facts about an organization – its profitability over the past few years, the number of people it employs – without some inside information.

The only real way to discover the realities of a company's management policy is to talk to the staff and hope for an objective appraisal. But getting to meet them, without a personal contact, can be difficult.

Try to meet as many people as possible at your interview. You'll be thought of as concerned and responsible if you ask to talk to members of the department you're destined for. Make sure that the Personnel director isn't present.

Ask them about:
- The throughput of actual work.
- Your everyday duties.
- The amount of liaison with the board.
- Arrangements for meetings.
- The implementing of decisions.
- Their own happiness and job satisfaction.

Q

My company is large, self-reliant and inward looking; all our courses and contracts are internal. I've been here five years and am afraid of losing all sense of the broader business world. Should I leave or immerse myself in the group culture?

Why leave? Business empires are rarely as black as they're painted.
- IBM never brought in another company or sold off parts of itself, and they've prospered. Their management trainee system has become a byword for excellence in business apprenticeship, without any reference to the outside world.
- Marks & Spencer developed a quality control system that is the envy of the international retail community without wondering what other companies were doing.

If your company is self-reliant, paternalistic, loyal to its 'family' of employees, solidly hierarchical and financially stable – if it's a genuine 'corporation' on the Japanese 'one-job-for-life' model – it's a splendid place to learn business skills first hand. Why worry about group culture? Accept what the company offers in home-grown wisdom and use it to become a better manager.

Q

I hear rumours that my company is heading for trouble. How can I tell if they're true? If they are, what should I do?

You could try to get access to the accounts, but they will be far from up-to-date.

You could have a chat with a manager from the finance department, and voice some departmental worries of your own in the hope of something in return, although it will still be difficult to obtain a clear picture.

All you can do is look for the danger signs. Does the company have:
- Out-of-date production methods?
- Dissatisfied customers?
- Late deliveries?
- A diminishing share of the market or a strong new competitor?
- Low profit margins and low volume?
- Dependence on a few suppliers/customers?
- Poor industrial relations/dissatisfied employees?
- High turnover of staff?
- Centralized decision making by a top-heavy management?

If you can answer yes to more than three of these, the chances are that the company *is* heading for trouble. You may be concerned enough to try and force changes.

If you feel the situation's beyond redemption, it would be better to leave.

Q

I'm constantly busy yet I never seem to get enough done. How can I organize myself better?

Remember Parkinson's Law: work expands to fill the time available for its completion. First of all, analyze your workload. See if you are doing anything that:

● Need not be done.
● Could (or should) be done by others.
● Wastes your time and abilities.

If there's still too much on your plate, you must learn to delegate to an assistant. If you're being given tasks to do for a superior, rather than problems to solve your own way, something has gone wrong; you can justifiably refuse some tasks. If part of the workload seems unnecessary, then say so. You mustn't be afraid to say no – while giving your reasons.

First, get organized. The detailed forms of time management will be dealt with more fully in turn, but here's a checklist of how to smarten up your *modus operandi:*

● Decide which tasks are crucial to the company's well-being, or have the highest promise of personal kudos. They're the ones which deserve your greatest concentration and attention. Divide the others into three or four descending categories of importance or urgency.

Cover everything. Now you'll be able to allot a certain amount of time to each task.

● At the bottom of the scale should be the routine, workaday tasks that come around every month (letter writing, admin, etc). If you can't delegate them, set yourself a regular time (in a dull part of the day) in which to carry them out. Decide what is your 'prime time' or 'A Time', and keep it closely guarded for your most important tasks.

● Allow yourself some time each day for personal rumination, creative thought and mental relaxation. According to the stress medics, you should be able to switch off for 15 per cent of your working time.

● Don't try to do too much. Don't neglect putting some time aside in your schedules for considering your home life.

● Remember that if you can manage your own time well, you can make sure those you manage are operating at maximum efficiency. Once you've done that, you can move on to the jackpot – improving the performance quality of your superiors.

Q

I have at least 50 different tasks to perform by the end of the month. How do I set priorities and allot the right amount of time to each?

Time is the most valuable resource you have, after people; and time limits the vital components of managerial control.

The typical manager's workload is a combination of:

1 Important, money-spinning, high-profile, long-term projects.
2 Medium-range creative activities such as writing reports and initiating work-improvement schemes.
3 Innumerable small-scale tasks that are predictable and niggling but nonetheless have to be done.

Unclassifiable in this line-up are the verbal interactions – meetings, telephone calls, presentations, reprimands, praise, one-to-one assessments and *ad hoc* chitchats in the corridor. Time must be found to accommodate them all.

Tasks in these three categories should be allotted work time in direct proportion to their importance.

Category Three items could, for instance, be lumped together and dealt with in a single blitzkreig lasting an hour, or might sensibly be delegated to a subordinate.

Category Two items generally require a full day's total immersion to 'break the back' of the problem or write the lion's share of the report, after which half a day might be given over to burnishing, editing, etc.

Category One items usually gestate over a period and require multiple delegations, staff meetings, progress analyses, crisis contingencies and the like. They deserve your fullest attention, concentration and time. They are the focus of your working life, the context in which you will most clearly be seen and assessed.

How do I decide the relative importance of two activities?

Ask yourself which carries the higher success profile. Carrying out a delicate operation efficiently may get you bonus marks with the board. But initiating action, going for a bold sales or cost-cutting campaign, seeing it through with flair and displaying that you're an effective operator will do a great deal more for your standing.

You must be tough and career-minded about this. Leave the information processing and number crunching to the bureaucrats on the staff.

You're trying to impress, to lead, to be in charge and stay there.

When should I tackle the various bits of work and ensure that everything gets done?

Simple answer: comprehensive planning and deadlines. Make sure nothing is left to chance, not even the smallest details. Writing copious lists, erroneously regarded as an activity typical of the neurotic, is in fact an invaluable exercise. Then it's a matter of deadlines:
● Give your delegates final dates (with 48 hours' contingency time thrown in) and demand they observe them.
● Make and remake timetables, endlessly tightening up the process.
● Shift deadlines around if you must, but only those well in advance of the Final Trump.

It's up to you when you tackle the day's tasks; most management advisors are adamant that you must start straight in at 9.05 with the first Category One file available, and never waste time on lesser items.

Perhaps you're the kind of person who can't happily open a serious project file until you've cleared away an hour's worth of trivia and know you won't be bothered about it again. Maybe it's only a form of managerial throat clearing – but it pays off if it gets you started on the Big Stuff.

Q

My workload varies. Some weeks I don't have enough to do, others I'm overburdened. What can I do to smooth things out?

Is the problem caused by inefficiency at the stage immediately before you? Does the occasional mountain of work mean a log-jam in a different department? Have you checked to see if the stack of paperwork that's come your way really needs dealing with, and needs to be dealt with by you? And if it is all relevant, can its arrival not be staggered across the weeks?

The real problem, I suspect, is in front of you rather than behind you: your delegating procedure. Clearly you're keeping too many jobs of a certain kind for yourself (a notorious and often chronic condition of the worried new manager), and disposing of too many of the others. It's a heady experience, sloughing off dull tasks to other people, but the more you diffuse the work, the less control you'll have over it.

Draw up two columns, one of the staff under your command and another of the work to be done in any given week or month, and ask:
● Are you matching the creative and the pedestrian workers to the right jobs?
● How are you assigning the tasks connected to important projects?
● Are you expecting three different activities from one person by the end of the month, or the same activity across three projects?
● Are you hogging all the marketing campaign planning, or are you letting the sales, design and R & D teams have a say in it?
● Are there certain tasks which crop up every month regularly which could be performed at any time? Fine. Give them to the new recruit. He/she will be grateful.

Q

My telephone is constantly ringing and members of staff are popping in and out of the room all day. How do I find time to myself without cutting my lines of communication?

You clearly need a crash course in the art of screening. You must start by getting a secretary or broadening the duties of the one you have. A crucial three-part function of a secretary's job should be to:
1 Intercept telephone calls and switch them through to you only if convenient. You can then decide how urgently you need to speak to colleagues; put off chatty friends; buy some time to marshal information if it's a superior ringing with an enquiry – or simply ignore the whole human race if you're feeling out of sorts.
2 Return calls which are simple requests for details of figures, invitations, suggested appointments, etc.
3 Help organize your time by steering would-be personal callers toward more suitable times in the day. Ideally your secretary might say 'He's busy right now. Can you come by at 11.30? James and the designers will be here then, so you can compare notes on progress.'

Q

My subordinates are in and out of my office in droves, seeking reassurance. How can I supervise their work while getting on with my own?

Look at your assessment procedures to make sure you aren't over-supervising their work. Alternatively, your delegating skills may have run away with you, so that you are producing unnecessary work to create an illusion of busyness.

You should have by your desk a large flow-chart of the department's work/output/product. It should be divided into separate project areas, which should themselves be subdivided into the individual operations of the staff. If you keep an eye on the macro-scale plan, you'll be better able to assess individual work requirements and appropriate deadlines at the personal level.

When people know what they're doing and have set deadlines, they'll stop coming to you for constant reassurance.

Q

Our office is fairly free and easy about time. We trust people to work a full day. What can I do about people who arrive late and go home early?

Bad timekeeping is a serious offence in the modern business world. But rather than being mere wilfulness, it's very likely to be a problem of motivation. Mr B. is dragging his heels to work because he doesn't like his supervisor, doesn't understand the new system that's been introduced, is conducting a vendetta with the person at the next desk, or is terminally bored with the work he does. If he persistently goes home early, he either hasn't enough work to do or else is rushing through it in his anxiety to get back to the crisis that's preoccupying him.

Talk to Mr B. It's the only way to find a solution that will suit you both. Call the errant employee into your office for a formal chat. Begin by asking how he gets to work, whether the journey is excessively long at present, whether he's recently moved house. Remark that it's been noticed he works unusual hours, and suggest you'd like to help. You might even suggest he considers job-sharing, if it's really impossible for him to get in any earlier.

If it is a matter of public transport, he'll be grateful for your attention. If not, you'll scare the life out of him. Ask what's wrong. Is it the job? Would he like to move to a different section? Is it the people? Is it the mid-life crisis? Is there trouble at home? Explain gently but firmly that, while you appreciate the real nature of his trouble, latecomers will sooner or later receive a private, then an official warning.

It's as simple as that. Your job as manager is to uncover the source of the trouble and see if the poor timekeeper's performance can be improved by judicious interdepartmental action. But make sure everybody knows the penalties for wasting the company's valuable time.

Q

How do I demonstrate to my staff that my time is precious and not to be wasted?

If you really want to get tough, you must get yourself an office and guard the threshold like a watchdog. If you like, close the door and hang a 'Do not disturb' sign on it (although this may lead to speculation that you are asleep or worse . . .).

Don't, of course, leave your door shut all the time. This is the Howard Hughes School of Management approach and makes very few friends.

Better, make a point of telling staff that between 3.30 and 4.30 is really not a good time to call, ever; although if they were to try between 12 and 1, any day, they'd be much more welcome and would find the door open. You'll sound as if you're simply suggesting appropriate times, but the times will be indelibly scorched on the memories of your subordinates (and will very likely be passed on to others).

Establishing that you have a 'Maximum Intensity' period and a 'Maximum Informality' period will show your subordinates they're dealing with a serious and time-conscious executive.

When staff ask to come and see you, make sure you find out what they want – just the subject, not the problem:

● Is the Post Room going on strike?
● Is it executive stress?
● Is it a personal problem?
● Is it to clarify your inexact instructions?

Then make an instant decision as to how long you can spend on this type of enquiry. Counting back from lunch or your next appointment, ask your subordinate to come 'in ten minutes', or 'in half an hour'. You won't be indicating directly how much of your time the problem is worth – but the message that you're conscious of the value of time will be clear.

Q

I like to arrive at a client's office about 10 minutes before the time we arranged to meet. I believe it shows willingness and hyper-punctuality and creates a good impression. Does it?

No it doesn't. Being early isn't the same as being punctual. What are you doing with ten minutes to spare? Do you assume the person you've come to see will drop everything and shift his schedule to accommodate you? Are you desperately anxious about seeing him? Is he, perhaps, your only client? See how you can put yourself at a disadvantage by being slightly too eager to please.

Being ultra-precise is the secret of creating an impression. Make an appointment for a precise time (rather than 'about 3 o'clock') and turn up on the dot – to the second if you can. Tell the chairman he'll get your report by '9.35 am.' rather than 'tomorrow morning' or 'by lunchtime'. That way you can convince everyone that this is how you operate in every department.

I'm a time-conscious manager, so I use the telephone as much as possible. Am I really saving time?

A telephone call is not always the quickest way of dealing with a problem.

Before you make a call, satisfy yourself that you are not consciously wasting time by calling someone you know will prolong the conversation and dissipate your concentration for the next half hour.

Lengthy descriptions of irrelevant personal matters, professional gossip, or whatever, are time consuming.

Several of my colleagues think nothing of dropping by at my office for a personal chat. How can I limit the time they spend sitting in my room?

Territorial psychology is the best way of handling the Corridor Cruisers.

If someone comes into your office unannounced, treat it as though some crisis must be imminent. Come out from behind your desk, so the intruder gets no further into the room, and deal with him/her standing beside the door. Don't give them the chance to start feeling at home.

If there's a knock at the door, go *outside* to see what it's about. This will imply that the inner sanctum is (a) busy, (b) exclusive to yourself, (c) a place where only serious work gets done, and (d) not to be invaded by trivia.

Chatterers can't be avoided entirely, and you would be an unpleasant individual not to like the occasional exchange of confidences. But do it on your own terms. When they approach you, say 'I'm terribly busy right now – can I come and talk about it in half an hour?' By going to their offices, you get what you like from them, while retaining the power to cut short the meeting when you wish.

How do I get rid of people without appearing rude?

Getting people to just GO requires directness but not much diplomacy. You don't even need to make excuses of the 'Must go, I promised to ring the Minister/wife/suppliers at 4.15' variety.

Conclude informal chat sessions by saying, 'I'm going to have to throw you out now because . . .'

Q

A member of my staff has pointed out that the company wastes vast amounts of stationery and that the copying machine is used unnecessarily. My time is too valuable to make a detailed investigation but I feel I should take some action. What?

Every office wastes paper; it's one of the facts of business life. Time spent on reducing costs is worthwhile. And a surprisingly large amount can be done about wastage, provided you instigate the right initiatives.

Issue a memo to every member of staff explaining that you are trying to save paper.

MEMORANDUM

TO: ALL MEMBERS OF STAFF

We are trying an experiment in paper conservation. Please abide by these rules:

1. In future, all memos will be kept short. Churchill used to ask his staff to brief him on complex troop movements using a maximum of one side of a single sheet of paper. We shall apply the same principle.

2. In future, memos will not be written on white A4 bond or Conqueror vellum. We shall use all recycled material – redundant company notepaper or the reverse side of old press releases, for example.

3. Factual enquiries seeking factual answers don't need a written memo. Use the telephone. You'll get an answer more quickly.

4. Never use envelopes for inter-office communication. If privacy is required, use a stapler. Better still, go and talk.

5. Invitations to corporate functions, head office gatherings and the like don't require a letter of acknowledgment. Accepting or turning down by telephone doesn't offend against etiquette.

6. Headed compliments slips are not glorified notepads. Don't use them unless in the course of a transaction with someone from outside the company.

7. An exercise book and pencil will henceforth be found on the photocopying machine. Please write in it the date, your name and department and the number of copies you have made. There will be a monthly audit to see which areas of our operation are using the machine most and least.

Q

Board room lunches usually start, with drinks, at midday and end at around 4 pm. How can the bosses set such a bad example and expect the workers to restrict themselves to one hour for lunch?

How indeed? Although the four-hour executive lunch, in-house or otherwise, is becoming less popular in the West, as the image of the fat capitalist gradually yields to that of the lean, breakfast-meeting infotech whizzkid, it still exists in older and more comfortable companies.

Clearly the long lunchers are setting a bad example of indolence and self-indulgence to their employees, but they can, and do, justify their behaviour. It's a matter of how much an individual contributes to the total revenue accruing to the company. A junior executive will be in a position to net the company a certain amount and no more – he/she is therefore paid £x,000 against the expectation of bringing in £3x,000 or £4x,000. If this projected revenue is costed on a daily basis, one can reach the magic figure of what a person's time is worth per minute.

The MD or chairman of a company, backed up by all its assets – stock, goodwill, operating and investment income – can, in a matter of minutes, make deals, or take decisions, that are worth vastly more to the company than any work output of the junior staff. The top people's minute-by-minute value to the company is proportionately greater – hence the amount of time they need spend engaged in actual work is proportionately less. In this context, such things as long lunches and late starts simply don't matter. But it remains a rather gross reminder to staff that the bosses inhabit a different orbit from theirs.

Q

I spend a great deal of time walking around the building to see the teams for which I'm responsible. Is this valuable or wasted?

Who do you think you are? John Egan? Sir Hector Laing? Walkabouts are the province of the paternalistic Top Men at Jaguar and United Biscuits, not the hardworking middle manager.

Get your subordinates to come to you, in groups or whole teams, at prearranged times, to discuss the latest stages of their work, present progress reports, raise any problems and answer your searching enquiries. That way, both they and you can be sure you know what's going on, without flannel or time-wasting on minor points. Doing it the other way round – the manager poking his/her nose into the minutiae of the processes – leads to diffusion, not progress.

The operating departments should know how to run themselves, to produce what they're scheduled to produce. All their energies should be focused toward you, and therefore toward the company's goals. Remember you're not a spectator of the department's work, you're the coordinator – the sharp end of the departmental arrowhead.

Teams and groups **62–5**   *Social occasions* **124–5**   *Company reports* **128–9**

Q

How do I find out just how busy I really am?

There's only one way to do this – and it can be most revealing.

Get a colleague, or a secretary who shares your office, to keep a detailed record of your activities over a single day. It needn't be minute-by-minute scrutiny: checks every half hour will be enough to get an impression. It's imperative that you do not know the day it will be – ask him/her to do it 'sometime in the next two weeks'.

Ask them to itemize the time devoted to each activity, however trivial:
● Phone calls.
● Absences from your desk.
● Meetings.
● Visits to the loo.
● Writing.
● Staring into space.

They should include when you arrive and depart, and what time you go to lunch and come back. They must glean, from innocent questioning, exactly what you are working on at any one time.

This is a potentially embarrassing but very revealing exercise in self-knowledge. You'll be surprised how your thrusting management style and breezy, decision-making flair is interspersed with daydreaming, gossiping and walking about.

Q

Try as I may, there always seems to be a cascade of paper covering my desk. Sometimes I can't find important documents in the morass. Is it my filing that's at fault, or me?

Some people find they can only work in the middle of a reassuring muddle; that if they haven't got all the relevant information on their desk, they'll lose it, or forget it and never get the job done. This is a bad attitude. Muddled desks lead to muddled thinking. The plethora of information sprawled in front of you usually proves counter-productive, if only in distracting you from individually manageable tasks.

Try out one of the more sensible apophthegms taught at American business schools: Never handle a piece of paper more than once. When incoming paperwork has been grouped into separate 'project files' on or around your desk, it must be processed as soon as possible. Pick up each sheet of paper with the firm intention of acting on it – not just shifting it back and forth. Do something with it:
● Pass it on to accounts or to Personnel.
● If it's a memo, reply to it on the same piece of paper (thus keeping it short and clear).
● Decide it's worth keeping and mark it 'File' for your secretary's attention.
● Simply throw it away and forget about it.

If you're chary of throwing away potentially important material, don't just add it to your ever-growing pile of marginal documents. Put a third tray alongside the 'In' and 'Out' trays, and mark it 'Hold, then Lose'.

Q

I'm told the morning is the best time for original or creative work, and the afternoon best for more routine, 'processing' paper-work. Is this true?

It's impossible to say. Every person works to his or her own rhythm. Some get tremendously wired up in the hour before going-home time, some do their best work from just after their first cup of coffee, but start to fade before lunchtime.

It isn't only to use the early morning light that film crews begin shooting (and film actors acting) at daybreak. And it is significant that Anthony Trollope and Arnold Bennett completed the lion's share of their daily word output by breakfast. Post-lunch fatigue, contrariwise, makes this a more obvious time to deal with boring workaday items such as schedules and replies to memos. But there are no rules applicable to everyone. What you need to do is to identify your prime time and use it profitably.

Q

I know I'm hard-working and conscientious, but there are times when I simply drift off, stare out of the window and daydream. How can I convert these periods from wool-gathering into concentration?

You're being too hard on yourself. It's simply impossible for the human mind to operate at full stretch all the time, and the periods of mental slackness you worry about are the equivalent of safety valves in the brain.

It's a much-quoted statistic in American business schools that 80 per cent of useful work is done in just 20 per cent of the time available. This is sometimes known as the 'A Time', the periods when the brain is most receptive, clear and creative. It's when decisions are taken most easily and you move convincingly from being a process-manager into

becoming a leader.

But this doesn't mean the less-important time periods are wasted, nor that your day-dreaming gathers only wool. Every manager needs to clear a space in each day in which to stop working.

Rather than let it just happen to you, why not consciously set aside a specific time each day – say 15 minutes between larger tasks – to ponder, reflect, assess, and indulge in a little creative free association. You're likely to achieve a greater sense of perspective about your work than you would have gained by continuing to slave away for that quarter hour.

% OF TYPICAL WORKWEEK SPENT ON VARIOUS ACTIVITIES

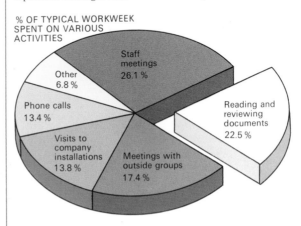

Staff meetings 26.1 %

Other 6.8 %

Phone calls 13.4 %

Reading and reviewing documents 22.5 %

Visits to company installations 13.8 %

Meetings with outside groups 17.4 %

Results of a survey of Chief Executive Officers by Fortune *magazine.*

Q

My secretary keeps a sharp eye on my appointments, lunches and other engagements. Is it necessary for me to keep a diary as well?

Undoubtedly yes; the question is what kind of diary.

Your bulky desk diary is fine for keeping a note of engagements via your secretary. But you must be independent of it. You must retain the ability to make or break dates without constant reference to your secretary. Nothing is more irritating than listening to a businessman say, over the dessert, 'Get your people to ring my people . . .'

A small, slim, light, one-week-per-page record-keeper is ideal. There's no need to go for those thick and elaborate tomes full of time zones in Antarctica and first-growth claret listings. It should be easily flicked in and out of your pocket, to provide constant reassurance about how your time is being spent, what you're doing, where you're going and who you're seeing next.

In addition to a pocket diary, the use of a 'time system' diary (page 40) is well worth considering. If you can't afford one, try a home-made system for setting priorities.

Q

I have innumerable day-to-day tasks which I have to fit around regular assignments. How can I decide what to do first?

Try this home-made system:
1 Find some old business cards and write on the back of each one a task you have to do.
2 Make two piles of cards: one of one-off jobs and one of recurring assignments (such as the regular Tuesday production meeting).
3 Put the one-offs in order of priority and slip them into clear plastic wallets (the kind that photo dealers sell for storing colour transparencies).
4 Do the same with the routine assignment cards.
5 Keep the two sheets face to face in a binder.
6 Complete the one-off tasks from the top, cross out the reminder information or make a note of any follow-up, then move those cards to the bottom of the sleeve.

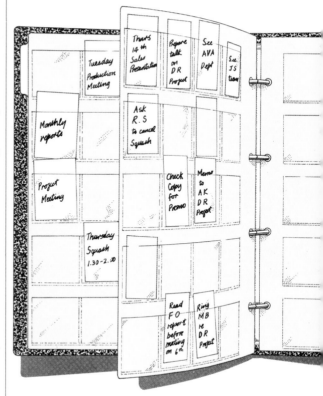

7 Use the same cards, and the same day at the office, to isolate the jobs you can delegate.

8 Put them into a third plastic sheet to prompt the briefings you must initiate on the next working day. Use it to control the monitoring of their completion.

You may convince yourself you *can* afford a 'time system' diary.

Q

I have my working day itemized in half-hour periods, and know exactly what's happening to my time. My appointments are minutely scheduled so that not a minute is wasted. Do I get a pat on the back?

Not yet. What happens when a meeting goes on 20 minutes longer than you'd planned? What if your secretary is off sick? What if your car breaks down? What will be the domino effect of a single minor crisis that affects every other part of your day?

Over-schematizing is a neurosis that can work against efficiency. You need to build some flexibility into the system. You need some contingency time. Think of the spare moments between meetings, phone calls, reports and administration as the gaps between railway lines that allow them to expand and contract as the atmosphere requires and ensure the trains can run in all weathers . . .

Q

What's so special about a ring-binder type of diary such as 'Filofax' and how can it help me?

Its special quality is to represent a portable database covering every aspect of your life. And at the end of the year you can keep the sections which haven't dated, and simply replace the loose-leaf diary.

Within the ring binder, the following sections are available:
● Personal data (account numbers, car details, insurance, passport, medical statistics, etc).
● Loose-leaf diary (each double-spread page represents a week).
● Fold-out 'year planner'.
● Bulky 'notepad'.
● Information section.
● Personal finance section for monitoring your weekly or monthly expenditure.
● Address book.
● Plastic wallet for credit cards, driving licence and even money.

The obvious danger of this system is that, should you lose it, your life will be in ruins for a couple of weeks or more.

While ring-binder diaries provide you with information in a readily retrievable form, they won't be of conspicuous help in making better use of your time.

Q

What are 'time system' diaries and how can they help me?

'Time system' diaries are the most sophisticated and elaborate means of monitoring your work output hour by hour, planning the most complex projects ahead, letting you see how your daily tasks are all part of a larger corporate goal, and encouraging you to decide the priorities of your life both at work and at home.

The diaries consist of a ring binder, a boxful of forms to be added or removed as the user wishes, and reams of ancillary graphs, flow charts and financial ledgers. The forms range from annual plans (a large rectangular grid on which long-term projects can be plotted week by week) down to daily plans, in which everything you do is monitored in half-hour segments. Thus the user can relate every part of a day's work to much wider contexts of time.

To begin with, it takes a lot of determination and discipline to fill in all the appropriate entries *and* make the required lists – but the act of writing down all your immediate requirements, tasks and activities is certainly salutary.

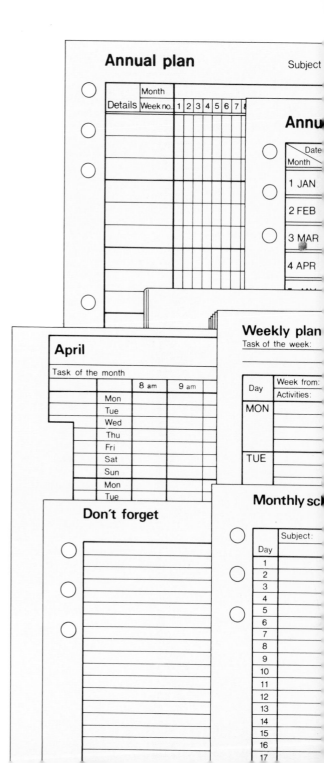

40

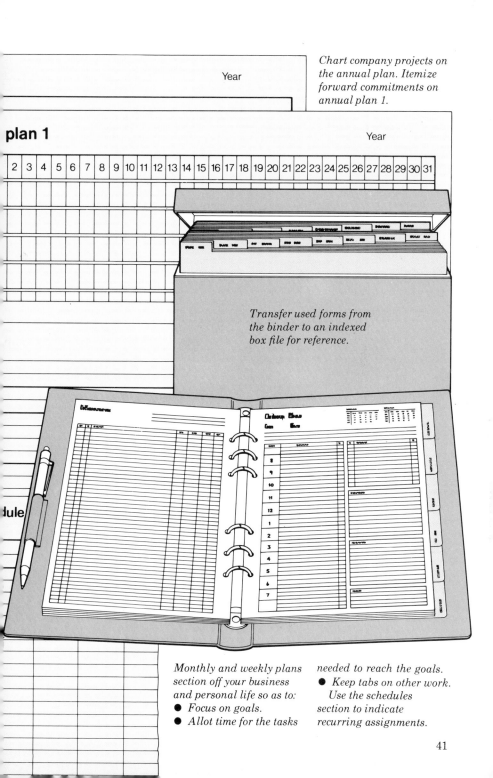

Year

Chart company projects on the annual plan. Itemize forward commitments on annual plan 1.

plan 1

Year

2	3	4	5	6	7	8	9	10	11	12	13	14	15	16	17	18	19	20	21	22	23	24	25	26	27	28	29	30	31

Transfer used forms from the binder to an indexed box file for reference.

dule

Monthly and weekly plans section off your business and personal life so as to:
- *Focus on goals.*
- *Allot time for the tasks needed to reach the goals.*
- *Keep tabs on other work. Use the schedules section to indicate recurring assignments.*

Q

I have just been promoted from the sales force, to become a manager. I know that I am a good listener and persuader and get on well with people. What other skills should I cultivate?

It's sensible of you to have started by analyzing your strengths.

The basic secret of effective and time-efficient self-management is threefold:

1 Knowing what you're good at.

2 Knowing what you can do.

3 Knowing what you can't do.

To identify these, think about what you like doing. What you do best will turn out to be, coincidentally, a similar activity.

If you enjoy writing detailed reports, or plotting flow charts, or making sales projections, plan to get better, more creative, thorough and efficient at each of them.

If you desperately dislike analyzing Balance Sheets, you must either delegate such work every time it appears, or make a special effort. In other words, try everything – once you become good at it you may find that you enjoy it.

Q

What qualities do I need to develop to become an efficient and successful manager?

Identifying the ideal qualities of today's manager is a thankless task, although hundreds of commentators have tried it.

Rosemary Stewart's excellent *The Reality of Management* cites an American survey of 'executive qualities' which homes in on no less than 15: 'Judgment, initiative, foresight, flair, energy, drive, human relations skills, decisiveness, dependability, emotional stability, fairness, ambition, dedication, objectivity and cooperation.'

But these inspiring ideas are hard to translate into practicalities. You can decide to take the initiative or to be more decisive but you can't resolve to wake up tomorrow as a more energetic or dependable person. However, there are realistic targets you can set. A manager should aim to be:

1 Endlessly flexible in getting along with all kinds of people.

2 Possessed of above average knowledge of modern technology.

3 Able to read a Balance Sheet with intelligence and insight.

4 Able to concentrate for short periods at maximum intensity.

5 Possessed of rat-like cunning and a sense of humour.

Being a tough self-seeker helps but it doesn't guarantee success. It may even work against advancement, leaving you without friends or allies when you need them. On the other hand, being everybody's friend doesn't mean that you'll automatically be picked for key posts.

An excellent piece of management wisdom is: 'The secret of success lies in having the power to convince other people that it is in their best interests to further your own.'

Q

I want to suggest to my colleagues that we try an entirely new method of bringing together design, production and marketing inputs at an early stage, and thus reduce departmental arguments and time wasted on non-projects. How do I go about introducing it?

Good for you – taking initiative and carrying your idea through will identify you as a skilled manager.

Your innovation must be an improvement on old procedures if it is to be effective. Anything else is just changing the *status quo* for its own sake, and will neither exercise your skills nor bring you advancement. Your idea must have genuine, consistent and quantifiable effects on the prevailing process. To carry it through depends on your drive and skills of persuasion as well as a receptive senior management.

Don't start with the top brass, however. Enlist the help of one or two colleagues. Discuss the idea with them to help you anticipate the criticism and questions that will come, in turn, from your superiors.

Results are the most important factors – so make sure that they are clearly defined and explained, drawn up on a game-plan with any charts, diagrams or other visual aids you can muster.

With your plan worked out, speak to your boss. Explain your idea and show him/her your supporting material. Tell him that you have formed a 'quality circle' with your colleagues to assess the feasibility of the new working method. It would take a hard-bitten boss not to be impressed by that – but don't become precious about your theory. Accept that your boss will pick holes in it. What matters is whether or not the final result has his whole-hearted support.

Next, the idea must be put to the board. Ask your boss to include it on the agenda for the next meeting, perhaps calling you in to explain the system's wider implications.

You must be ready for opposition that will seem illogical or perverse; and for stubborn resistance that expresses itself in criticizing the timing or the personnel or quite extraneous logistical details. Don't despair. These are the professional nay-sayers who would rather see the company in genteel collapse than in the throes of innovation.

Persuade the board to accept a special committee report on the new approach. These findings will carry infinitely more clout than your own insistence. Make sure that all three departments are fully represented and allowed to contribute their own suggestions. This way, your idea will penetrate to a new echelon where people will want to be seen giving responses and making sensible contributions to your plan.

Finally, you must follow the idea through. When everyone considers it as exciting as yesterday's papers, you must continue to galvanize your colleagues into action until it is successfully implemented.

Remember that bureaucracy and boredom are the two elements most inimical to the successful introduction of the new.

Q

Now I'm the manager of our purchasing division, I'm expected to go on management training courses and weekend jaunts designed to develop my leadership skills. I think it's a waste of time. Is it?

Management courses aim to improve, through clarification of objectives and methods, your day-to-day operations.

Some executives take management training extremely seriously, find it stimulating and are able to apply their newly acquired wisdom on their return to the company. Others find the whole atmosphere rather too scholastic or full of fake cameraderie.

The best thing to do if you want to know how management theory might help you to develop your management skills is to attend a one-person seminar: buy or borrow a management training film made by a company such as Video Arts. If it entertains you and no more, fine. If you feel you cannot learn from it, the chances are that you are just temperamentally indisposed toward change. But if it solves any problems, raises illuminating questions or suggests some technical skill you haven't tried before – you may become a regular on the training-course circuit.

Q

I've been with the company for five years, but I don't feel they're developing my talents sufficiently fast. Should I ask my boss when they are going to use some initiative, or should I look for a job elsewhere?

Why should it be up to the company to 'develop' your talents.

True management development is about self-discipline, self-starting, self-control and self-awareness. The acquisition of these qualities is beyond simple employee training and development schemes. You have to be responsible for your own advancement.

Start today. Confront your boss head-on and tell him/her you feel under-used, that you're sure you could be trusted with a project in a different area, or with a report that someone else is scheduled to write.

More difficult, although more rewarding, would be to suggest to your boss that you should move into a completely new area such as finance or computing, if that's where you feel your talents lie. Good bosses recognize the potential of willingness and enthusiasm, and encourage it.

The next step may be extra training (or on-the-spot coaching for technical information), enabling you to speak to whole new departments and strata of staff on an advanced level.

The way to get on is to take the initiative in improving your career path . . . not waiting for your fairy godmother to do it for you.

Self-improvement campaign

1 Learn as much as you can about the company and the industrial context within which it operates. Study its history and surmise about its future.
2 Get associated with public bodies connected with your work – a trade association for instance.
3 Find out who your opposite numbers are in rival companies. Find out who is doing the job best, and study his/her methods. Consider going for some refresher training. Talk to the

Q

I've been finance director of this company for three years, and marketing director for the last two. But when the chief executive's slot became vacant recently I was passed over in favour of a less-qualified board member. How much seniority do I need to get to the top?

Getting to the top is more than a matter of racking up seniority points and assuming you'll eventually hit the jackpot. It's predominantly to do with image – that indefinable piece of corporate style management that makes other people want to see you in charge.

Certainly you know about finance and marketing; you know about the company's presentation of its books and its products.

How about your presentation of yourself? How do you come across to employees who don't immediately know your title? As tough or malleable, go-ahead or pedestrian, heroic or banal, capable or neurotic, shrewd and watchful or gossipy and extravagant?

None of these is an inherent quality; all are outward expressions of implied psychological traits. And although their expression is hardly more than a matter of acting, image-projection can undoubtedly shift mountains.

As Quentin Crisp once wrote of the closely allied concept of charisma, 'It's the power to influence without the need for logic.' It's something you can't learn in a week, but you can work at it, burnish it, improve it, change it to fit. Plan a campaign of self-improvement.

opposition in a spirit of enlightened mutual help. Get your name known on the circuit.
4 Get academic. Read the magazines and learned journals connected with your work. Make up your mind about the moral, ethical or political issues touched by your industry's products or working methods. If you feel injustice or anomaly is in the air, take a stand against it.
5 Try to look the part. Take a serious look at your appearance. Is that dandruff? Are your shoes scuffed? Is your jacket/footwear/hemline/

tie hopelessly out of date? Consider getting a good-quality made-to-measure suit or an expensive dress to conceal executive spread. But don't get too trendy: you're seeking seniority, not trying to open a boutique.
6 Court the media. Try writing an article for a trade journal, keeping it general in nomenclature (no puffs for your company) but specific in recommendation. Once you start to sound like a pundit of the industry, you'll be gratefully treated as one. Get to meet local radio or TV people. Use your PR

office to fix up lunch with useful people – meeting you as equals.
7 Learn to take criticism. Your colleagues won't be thrilled to watch an old cynic like you turning into the Grand Old Man/Woman of the industry, and may snipe at you behind your back. Expect it – and make sure your judgments are sound and your pronouncements backed up by fact. Never assume the media will swallow waffle. Don't forget there's always another brilliant pundit waiting to take your place . . .

Company reports **128–9** *Profit and growth* **156–7**

Q

In my CV I stated that I spoke fluent Italian. Now my evenings are spent deep in the dictionary translating business letters from Milan received by other departments. Should I admit my lie or carry on the charade?

If the charade continues, it will undoubtedly get worse. From translating letters, you'll be invited to reply to them, in fluent Italian. When a business contact (or, worse, a customer) appears from Rome, you'll be detailed to entertain him or her over lunch – and that'll be like the Death By a Thousand Cuts. You can't go down that road.

The problem is how to extricate yourself without losing face.

Don't admit that you told a lie. Your bosses will start looking for other, as yet unrevealed, examples of your non-capacities.

Have a word with your immediate overseer and, with a lot of self-deprecating laughter, say that, well, you used to speak Italian, fluently, did a Bertlitz course for three months in 1979, spent three consecutive summers in Perugia, but seem to have got a bit rusty now.

Keep it lighthearted, and they'll never know just how much you bent the truth.

Q

I've been offered a better-paid job in a different department, but I'd rather hang on for the top position in my present department. Should I stay or go?

Finding the perfect balance between financial reward and job satisfaction always comes down to personal temperament.

You know better than anyone the kind of job you're happiest with – and the one in which, consequently, you perform best. Money, hard though it is to believe, comes a poor second to this vital matching up process.

But what do you see yourself doing in five years' time? In charge of the same department? Or working more broadly as a general manager, veteran of half-a-dozen departments and renowned as a Jack-of-all-trades achiever?

No one can say that one type of manager is better than another. The all-rounder will have width of reference in the management field but may lack in-depth knowledge of a particular area, while the one-trick artist may become the nation's Top (and highest-paid) Manager.

What's important is to understand which type suits your personality.

Establish your ambitions. Decide on the first in a (presumably) long line of 'life goals', in which you tell yourself exactly what position you will hold at some date in the future: 'By 1990, I shall be managing director of a different computer company, perhaps smaller than this one but with a sales emphasis on fifth-generation technology. I shall be earning four times my present salary and have a weekend cottage on the coast.'

Having performed this rather self-conscious exercise, you must work out the possible stepping stones to achieving your goal. Should you, for example:
● Rise through the ranks to become marketing director at 45, then move sideways?
● Move departments or jobs now to increase your bankability early on?
● Join a firm with a job-rotation programme to gain more experience?

Whatever you choose should move you constantly forward toward your life goal. Anything else is either pocket money, self-indulgence or flagrant time-wasting.

Q

How can I, a woman manager, be a feminist in a male business community without becoming fainthearted?

Adopt male traits and strategies? That's selling out to the opposition. Protest about every instance of thoughtless chauvinism? That'll get you labelled as a harridan. Meekly accept a second class position? Never.

It's a real problem sticking to your principles, stressing your rights and standing your corner in a male-dominated world. Is compromise the answer?

'You need never compromise,' says Jill Tweedie, leading feminist writer. 'A person who is absolutely sure of her ground will automatically make others understand that there are limits to behaviour. It's all done by body language, by exuding an absolute security.

'Everyone knows what's going on in human communications – you must make sure people get the message right from the start. You might try teaching yourself some basic truths, simply by saying: "I am a human being, I have dignity, I am equal to other humans, what other people have, I have myself."

'Protesting all the time about the way you're treated isn't really the way. Nor is accepting tokenism; even if you join Parliament, you do so only on male terms, start making male excuses for things and gradually become one of them.

'A woman who wants to get ahead must take other women along with her. Women need the support of other women if they are going to change business organizations for the better.'

Q

I'm feeling very bored with my job. Sure it earns me plenty of money, but I feel I'm just treading water. How can I get my old enthusiasm back?

Your enthusiasm was partly caused by a paradox: when you started the job, you felt subconsciously that it was slightly more than you could handle, but that you'd have a go anyway.

This is not a new phenomenon: Robert Browning wrote 'Ah but a man's reach should exceed his grasp/Or what's a Heaven for?'

Now you're well on top of the job, there's no challenge, no 'reaching' about it any more, and you see yourself as a well-paid shifter of over-familiar bits of paper and personnel.

You'll only get fired up in the old way by getting a new job. Be more ambitious. Stop thinking of your present treadmill and look for a responsible position in another department or another company if there's no obvious 'next place' in the hierarchy at your workplace. Don't tell yourself you are unable to climb higher.

What you need is an invigorating blast of impossible dreams.

Coping with stress 14–15   *Understanding your job* 24–5

Q

It's some time since I had to prepare a curriculum vitae for a job application. What guidelines are there to ensure maximum effectiveness?

Emphasize the positive; skate over the negative.

There's no need to list your school grades, your class of degree (unless it's a congratulatory First from Harvard or Oxford), nor all your music exams.
Get into the Experience section as soon as you can.

Emphasize your current job by giving it a separate heading.

For each job you've held, give the dates (just the year), the company's name, the position you occupied and a brief explanation of your duties. State your salary only if it shows a steadily rising curve through your career.

CURRICULUM VITAE

MATILDA JANE CASSIDY

Date of Birth:	24 October 1941.
Place of Birth:	Dublin, Ireland.
Personal Details:	Married with three sons and a daughter. Living in Greenwich, Connecticut, USA, and Hampstead, London.
Education:	1948-59 Ursuline Convent, Donnybrook, Dublin. 1960-63 St Anne's College, Oxford University. 1963-64 The City Business School.
Qualifications:	BA Hon (1st Class) in Politics, Philosophy and Economics. MBA with distinction in business law.
Present Occupation:	1979- Co-founder and chief executive, Total Woman Clothes shop chain (HQ address).
Business Experience:	1964-65 Junior Catering Executive, J. Lyons Ltd. 1965-67 Management trainee, Beechams Industries (address). (Experience of general line management) 1967-68 Freelance work for private clients. 1968-73 Marketing Manager, Pentos Group (address). (Headed 22-strong marketing team, covering five products from magazines to garden furniture) 1973-78 Sales and Marketing Director, Barnard Trust Inc. (Marketing consultant to international conglomerate, with special responsibility for launching Italian Stallion clothes-shop Franchise)

If you were once in a lowly job and are now ashamed of it, give it a formally euphemistic title. (You spent most of this year waitressing.)
Alternatively, you could present your jobs in reverse date order to highlight your recent record and to gloss over your humble beginnings.

Don't leave gaps unexplained. Massage the facts a little if the truth is too hard to bear. (You spent most of this time in a Haight-Ashbury commune.)

Achievements:	1972 Oversaw (as project coordinator) wholesale relocation of company to new Berkshire premises. 1976 Successful launch of menswear franchise. Masterminded export of chain to US: Queen's Award. 1980 Established 14-shop chain of own-brand women's wear. Successfully diversified into cosmetics and accessories. Opened three experimental outlets in New York, Florida and Los Angeles.
Honorifics:	Fellow of British Institute of Management. Fellow of Institute of Directors. 1983 Shortlisted for Veuve Cliquot Businesswoman of the Year Award. 1984 Visiting Fellow at Yale University (lecturing in Export Management and International Business). Member of Equal Opportunities Commission steering group.
Publications:	'Marketing in a Recession' (Klutz, 1973). 'Women On Top: the Female Boardroom' (Harridan, 1980).
Recreations:	Karate Black Belt (1st Dan). Flower Arranging. Kabuki Theatre.
Further Information:	UK address and phone number.
Enclosures:	Two letters of recommendation from previous employers.

Some commentators deprecate the idea of a section on 'Achievements' as being excessively egotistical. In fact, it is the only indication a putative employer will get of your real business achievements.

Take a separate line for each item and list the feathers in your cap.

Anything connected with the public sphere – membership of important societies, a book published, a yacht race won, a seat on a Government committee – should be added, together with any business awards.

Recreations should be as interesting as possible: say nothing rather than admit to 'Walking', 'Light gardening' or 'Watching TV'.

You must judge for yourself the efficacy of appending a series of letters from ex-employers and non-partisan onlookers who can corroborate your achievements. Some people find such correspondence mildly embarrassing, although they may help your case.

Your covering letter should:
● Formally apply for the position.
● Say where you heard of the job.
● Describe your current employment and explain its relevance to the job offered.
● Say why you want the job.
● Indicate your availability for an interview.

Q

I want to be chief executive of my own company by the time I'm forty. Should I get a firm grounding in finance now (at 27) or do an 'apprenticeship' in several managerial roles?

There aren't many hard and fast rules for the ideal career plan. But it's worth looking at the routes taken by the people who have made it to the top.

Many present-day managing directors, chairmen and chief executive officers start as accountants, while few get there via the Personnel department. Some have spent their whole working lives in one corporation; others have climbed the ladder by constantly 'moving house' and learning different specializations.

Every year the American magazine, *Fortune*, draws up a list of the 500 largest US industrial corporations ranked by sales. Its survey of America's top chief executive officers revealed the typical business magnate to be a 50-ish Catholic male from a small town in the Mid-West, who has held his current position for seven years, after a career which rarely spans more than four companies, works a 55–60 hour week and earns between $450,000 and $900,000 p.a.

The majority of CEOs hit the top post after working there for between 10 and 15 years, indicating that loyalty and solid hard graft pay dividends. Forty per cent of the bosses of industrial companies rose through engineering or

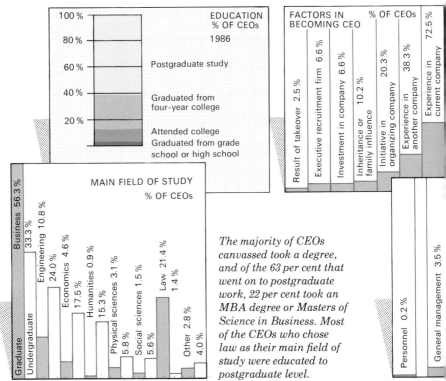

EDUCATION
% OF CEOs
1986

Postgraduate study

Graduated from four-year college

Attended college
Graduated from grade school or high school

FACTORS IN BECOMING CEO — % OF CEOs

- Result of takeover 2.5 %
- Executive recruitment firm 6.6 %
- Investment in company 6.6 %
- Inheritance or family influence 10.2 %
- Initiative in organizing company 20.3 %
- Experience in another company 38.3 %
- Experience in current company 72.5 %

MAIN FIELD OF STUDY
% OF CEOs

- Business 56.3 %
- Graduate 33.3 %
- Undergraduate
- Engineering 10.8 %
- 24.0 %
- Economics 4.6 %
- 17.5 %
- Humanities 0.9 %
- Physical sciences 3.1 %
- 5.8 %
- Social sciences 1.5 %
- 15.3 %
- 5.6 %
- Law 21.4 %
- 1.4 %
- Other 2.8 %
- 4.0 %
- Personnel 0.2 %
- General management 3.5 %

The majority of CEOs canvassed took a degree, and of the 63 per cent that went on to postgraduate work, 22 per cent took an MBA degree or Masters of Science in Business. Most of the CEOs who chose law as their main field of study were educated to postgraduate level.

production.

Perhaps most significant, more than half of the chiefs followed their comparatively wealthy fathers on to the management ladder.

A significant factor in Getting On is education. In the Western world, the academic businessman occupies a higher profile in the top ranks than the gifted, amateur whizzkid.

Fortune Magazine's survey reveals that sales and marketing are the disciplines with the highest pay-off for the ambitious executive, with finance a close second. Most of today's CEOs say that experience in one company is the key to promotion.

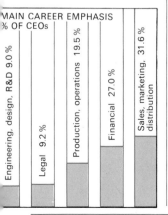

Q

I'm a manager in a large company which has been more than generous to me. I know I'll want to go it alone sooner or later. How do I work out the best timing?

Some people would say that once you've decided to go 'sooner or later' you've already gone.

Are you waiting to resign in the quiet period over the summer? Forget it: better to have your replacement thrown into the middle of the action.

Do you intend to pay the company back in some way for their goodness? The best way is to make your departure as smooth and well-anticipated as possible:
1 Tell your boss you plan to 'go it alone', say, three months' hence.
2 Discuss the current stage of all your projects and draw up a flow chart on each of them.
3 Indicate any current trouble areas and try to pinpoint possible future difficulties.
4 Tell the boss who you regard as the key departmental figure in terms of understanding and expediting the work you are in charge of.

The best 'timing' for going solo has nothing to do with your job, only with your future financial arrangements. Consult your bank manager not your boss.

Q

A colleague has just been headhunted for a key job in the industry's Number One firm. How can I get myself headhunted?

Many executives nowadays ask directly to be considered for jobs going in a specific field and above a certain executive level.

With the headhunters' files full of the names of executives, the best way to stand out is to make a name for yourself as a valuable source of information and character assessment.

Headhunters (or, more properly, 'executive search consultants') depend on information about the Right People. They welcome unprompted assistance. If you hear of a top job going unadvertised and can find out (via the company's Personnel manager) which search organization is involved, try calling them and putting a suitable candidate's name forward, provided it's not: (a) your own (vanity), nor (b) barefaced nepotism.

You'll be asked to identify yourself and, with luck, they'll call you for further advice.

It should be only a matter of time before a job in your field is offered directly to you instead of to another by way of your expert opinion.

MANAGING YOURSELF / WORKSPACE

Q

I'm hopelessly untidy and my office always looks a mess, though I always know where everything is. How can I reform?

If you're prepared to admit it's a mess, think how revoltingly obvious it must be to others. It's no good insisting you can only work in a muddle. A pigsty of papers, envelopes, staples and half-empty packets of biscuits affects morale, is bad for your image (no matter what results you may claim), and in a serious, all-embracing sense, is counter-productive.

Do you really always know where everything is? Managers who need to have 'everything' in front of them at all times give off sonic waves of instability. *Use the filing system.* Start your own if necessary, but get all the non-immediate paper off your desk. As long as you can trust your secretary, life will be much easier when you can press the intercom and say 'The Armfield File, please,' rather than spend anxious minutes scrabbling around for it.

Next, get rid of the non-essential hardware cluttering your desk. Keep the items you need every hour of every day. Get rid of the rest and trust your secretary to have a supply. You're a creative business dynamo, not a school-child with a satchel-load of trivia.

Try to take pride in the way you run your work life. As a manager, you're supposed to be methodical, precise, sharp and never at a loss. It's hard to feel that way when your surroundings are messy.

Q

I've inherited offices which are luxurious compared to those of my team members. Would it be good policy to even things out?

How? Sub-let them to your subordinates? Swop with members of the team on a rota basis? Give them back?

It makes no sense to feel guilty because, by virtue of being in charge, you inherit the trappings of power. The manager is not the anonymous administrator of some process dictated by another, but is in control, taking decisions, and giving orders.

If you're going to be the Henry Ford of the production department, start acting like it. And be thankful for any visible outward sign that you're deserving of more respect than others. Impose your personality on your offices and you'll start to feel, on reflection, that luxurious surroundings are no more than the due recognition of your unique talents.

Q

I'm the boss, but I like to be close to the office team. Should I just put a screen between us, or would it be better to have my own room?

Having your own room bestows the kudos appropriate to a boss. There's something a bit undignified about the top manager being seen to 'muck in' with the team. The price you have to pay, however, is the distance you put between yourself and the immediate workforce.

Working from the other side of a plaster screen is a slightly artificial form of privacy. A better solution, one that offers a combination of visibility and separate-ness, is to have a smoked-glass screen mounted in one wall of your office. Your staff can then establish whether you are:

- In or out.
- Busy or disturbable.
- In conference or alone.
- Watching them or not.

Q

I've been given an office of my own for the first time. It has a desk, a chair, a telephone and a bookcase but nothing else. To what extent can I impose my own personality on it?

A fascinating area of corporate image-making: the answer is to adopt a judicious combination of comfort and austerity, conventionalism and idiosyncrasy.

Nothing tells the outside world as much about you as the paraphernalia of your workspace. So be sober to an extent, to reassure superiors of your seriousness as an executive. And be stylish to show everyone that there's more to you than mere efficiency.

First, make sure your workspace helps you do your job. Don't clutter it with unnecessary material: consign anything that's fileable to your secretary. Get an 'In' tray and ask for inter-office papers to be left in the tray.

Naturally you want to work in comfort, so request an ergonomically-sophisticated chair that presses against the strategic points of your spine.

You need to avoid eyestrain, so have dimmers fitted to your room lights and a hinged lamp on your desk.

If the room is large, a sofa and a coffee table are potent status symbols, implying that, for some people, you're prepared to be informal and gracious; but use them sparingly. A second chair across the desk from your own is a necessity.

Framed pictures on the wall are *de rigueur*, but be careful not to alarm (or distract) visitors with anything too startling; or to betray a lack of imagination. Pirelli calendars were once the only acceptable displays of human flesh, but they're now defunct and would be considered sexist, anyway.

By all means, include a few well-designed personal items among the decorations, but cuttings from the papers with headlines featuring your name in some allegedly humorous context are strictly for the mailroom boys. So, too, are executive toys such as Newton's cradles.

Objets d'art must be discreet: some memento from a previous, triumphantly successful job is just about acceptable, provided nobody can accuse you of living in the past. Much better is something foreign, inanimate and in its natural state.

Desk accessories should be kept to a spare minimum and reassessed every so often.

Motivation **74–7** *Working conditions* **98–9**   53

Q

One of our financial supervisors is hard-working and efficient, but it is becoming clear to me that she is far from well. How can I help her?

Few things are more important to you as a manager than the health and well-being of your staff. No amount of career prospects compare with the importance of their good health. You should be aware of symptoms that could indicate that professional help is needed, even if work is not affected.

The first person with whom you should discuss the problem is the member of staff who is unwell, whatever his or her rank.

Reveal your concern by asking your financial supervisor:

1 Has she seen her GP for a check-up recently?

2 Is she receiving proper medication, on prescription?

3 Does she know if she is allergic to any food or drug?

4 Have personal or family problems aggravated a medical condition?

5 Does she find the present level of work a strain?

6 Would she benefit from a recuperative period of paid leave?

If you find out that she is receiving medical care, stop worrying. If not, suggest she sees the company doctor.

If that doesn't push her into helping herself, and her condition is deteriorating, you'll have to resort to being devious. Ask the MD to make an appointment for both of you to see the company doctor.

When she says 'I've been given an appointment with the doctor', you say 'Oh so have I. It must be a routine screening for our unit.'

Q

Some members of my staff belong to ethnic minorities and are being victimized. How can I stop this?

It's vitally important that any signs of incipient racism should be nipped in the bud, before the company is called before the Race Relations Board.

What form does the victimization take? If it's a question of some staff being unfairly saddled with the boring or dirty jobs, then it's up to you to reschedule the work so that everyone shares it equally, without prejudice or favouritism.

If it's more personal – amounting to verbal or physical abuse and innuendo – it's more serious, and requires direct action.

Ideally, you should act before the victims come to you with an official complaint. Try to identify the ringleaders and investigate a single incident with a sharp disciplinary interview.

Let it be known that you won't tolerate bigotry in the firm and that you're prepared to fire any perpetrator of such racism.

Don't treat the victimized differently – your job is to neutralize the bad feeling.

Q

I was appalled to learn that one of my staff uses cocaine. Should I remonstrate with him, or is it none of my business?

Mere possession of cocaine – let alone sniffing it or dealing in it – is a criminal offence. It can render the owner liable to heavy fines or imprisonment. This could reflect badly on the whole company.

In addition, cocaine is addictive, expensive and all-absorbing. If your colleague isn't yet an addict, he may soon become one. His work will suffer beyond repair as the drug becomes his only priority.

Call him in for a meeting, and demand to know what he proposes to do about his drug habit. Point out that, while you appreciate the value of his work, you've no place in the company for criminals or junkies.

If he makes light of the whole business, point out the dangers awaiting him. Give him a last warning, and be prepared to back it up with dismissal.

Q

My boss is always flirting with me, making comments on my 'figure' and suggesting that we run off together. Should I complain that I'm being sexually harassed?

Your boss may be a pest, a chauvinist and an oaf, but he's not guilty of sexual harassment in the usual sense. Harassment is when Person A actively prevents or hinders Person B from getting advancement or otherwise prejudices their position in the firm, solely because Person B will not indulge his/her sexual advances.

For the moment, there seems to be no question of sexual blackmail in your case.

Your boss probably means well, but he's a sexist and cannot communicate with a woman, except in physical terms. But this doesn't mean that you should tolerate his behaviour.

Try rounding on your boss and complimenting him on his beer paunch or receding hairline. Show your distaste at the idea of running anywhere with him. Be as direct as you need to stop his advances.

Rather than women needing assertiveness training, men might benefit from a course in sensitivity training.

Q

A valuable member of my staff has personal odour problems that are causing complaints. How do I get the message across tactfully and sympathetically?

Most managers dread the embarrassment of such a confrontation.

You can try to blame the trouble on errant central heating or hypersensitive colleagues, but eventually you are going to have to tell him he smells.

You can soften the blow by skirting round the question thus: 'Do you find it very hot in your office?' 'Are the washrooms satisfactory?' and so forth.

But finally you'll have to say 'I'm sorry but your clothes reek of sweat and people are beginning to notice. I'm sure it's because you perspire more than other people.'

The blunt approach is the only one. Reassure him, however, that his work is good and that he is a valuable member of the team. Then end by asking him to see if he can clean up his person.

If you cannot face this, or if the person is of the opposite sex, you will have to enlist the help of one of his/her friends.

Q

I have heard that my sales manager, who knows our plans for the next five years, was seen at lunch with the chairman of our main competitor. Should I try to find out why?

Yes, but they might simply be old friends so don't jump to conclusions. There could by several possible explanations.

Talk to your manager in private, steering the conversation to the rival firm and its top people. Mention the meeting, if necessary. He may claim it was a calculated bid to extract information. If you believe him, fine. Someone working for the company's good deserves approbation.

If you doubt his intentions, remind him that disloyalty is a sackable offence. Someone sabotaging the company deserves to be dismissed.

If you find out he's leaving, whether taking company secrets or not, don't lose any sleep over it. Most businesses have a good idea of what the opposition is up to.

Q

I share a filing cabinet with a colleague whose husband works for a rival organization. I must keep the project I'm developing secret. How should I proceed?

Don't get too paranoid, or you won't be able to work with your colleague at all. However, it may be wise to take a few elementary precautions:
● The greatest danger lies in your leaving the entire project in a single file for her inspection, so disperse the material. Keep costings separate from flow charts (file the former in an unspecified 'Budgets' folder; keep the latter locked in your briefcase), and interim reports separate from suppliers' specifications.
● Correspondence is the most obvious area where the whole project could be revealed. You should keep your letters locked in your desk as though they were personal.
● Use a shredder once you've digested material that's important but needn't be retained in hard-copy form.
● Only take essential photostats, one for each of the appropriate project executives.
● If you use a computer, put everything on to floppy disk, and leave no paper lying around.

Q

A member of my team claims to have finished the tasks assigned to her long before they are really done. Do I reprimand her for lying or accept this as a personal foible?

It is unlikely that there is anything sinister in this behaviour. She is probably trying to impress you with her efficiency.

On the other hand, her fantasy world of super-fast action will be less than helpful in a busy department where attention to both details and deadlines is important.

You need, therefore, to administer an oblique reprimand when next she claims to have 'finished' her work.
● Ask to see the work immediately.
● Appear to be putting yourself out to do so.
● Go with her to her office, if necessary.
● Ask to see the relevent figures or report.

Any of these approaches should shock her into reality. If her work *is* unfinished, your benign, uncritical questioning will dismay her and ensure that the behaviour is not repeated.

Q

There's a bad apple in our barrel. He's enormously talented, but he erodes the morale of everyone around him. How can I make him change?

There are times when it isn't quite enough to take individuals aside for a talk. The bumptious, the vainglorious, the obstreperous and the monomaniacal tend not to respond to the measured tones of good common sense. They will change only if the impulse to do so comes from within themselves.

Therefore, you should give him a hard time. Tease him, make his irritating quirks become office jokes, and make him aware of it. Show him that everyone knows his faults, and talks about them behind his back.

You can give the impression that his behaviour or his attitudes are really quite endearing – but have no compunction about making fun of them at the same time . . .

If he's too thick-skinned to alter his behaviour after that, at least you'll have made it clear to your staff that you realize how difficult he is to work with.

Q

I have been asked to write a reference for someone I sacked for incompetence. He's now desperate for a job. What is the correct approach?

You have to strike a balance between honesty and diplomacy.

There is no such thing as a bad reference. All references are deemed positive endorsements of their subjects' general skill. So if you think a person does not merit such an endorsement you must simply decline.

Provided your reasons for the sacking were sound, there is no reason why you should feel guilty about such a refusal, although it would be churlish to be impolite.

If you want to do something to help, anything on paper is better than nothing. The procedure here is to damn with faint praise.

Write simply that the person worked for you for a certain period in a certain capacity. Do not say anything about their effectiveness unless you sincerely mean it.

Remember that these documents are not confidential and you could risk legal recrimination by giving false information.

Q

You should never give an office thief a second chance – true or false?

True, I'm afraid. It's just not worth taking the risk. And there are no exceptions.

Q

I need to recruit a new member of staff to join my team but I'm concerned about the budget allocation for salaries. How do I establish that a new recruit is really needed and, if so, make sure I attract the right person?

Why has the vacancy arisen? Is it because:

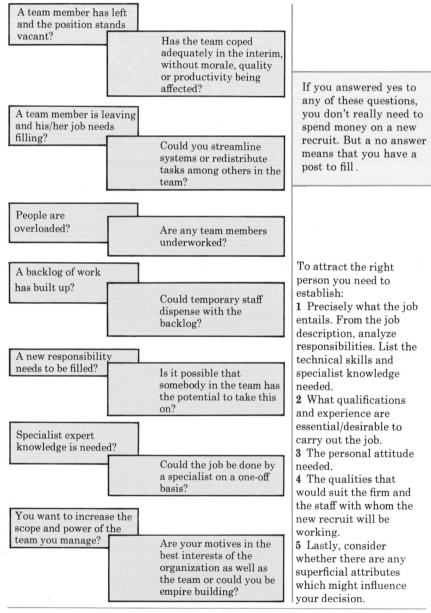

A team member has left and the position stands vacant?

Has the team coped adequately in the interim, without morale, quality or productivity being affected?

A team member is leaving and his/her job needs filling?

Could you streamline systems or redistribute tasks among others in the team?

If you answered yes to any of these questions, you don't really need to spend money on a new recruit. But a no answer means that you have a post to fill.

People are overloaded?

Are any team members underworked?

A backlog of work has built up?

Could temporary staff dispense with the backlog?

A new responsibility needs to be filled?

Is it possible that somebody in the team has the potential to take this on?

Specialist expert knowledge is needed?

Could the job be done by a specialist on a one-off basis?

You want to increase the scope and power of the team you manage?

Are your motives in the best interests of the organization as well as the team or could you be empire building?

To attract the right person you need to establish:
1 Precisely what the job entails. From the job description, analyze responsibilities. List the technical skills and specialist knowledge needed.
2 What qualifications and experience are essential/desirable to carry out the job.
3 The personal attitude needed.
4 The qualities that would suit the firm and the staff with whom the new recruit will be working.
5 Lastly, consider whether there are any superficial attributes which might influence your decision.

Q

How do I make sure that an interview tells me what I really want to know about a job applicant?

To assess a candidate's suitability, analyze his/her CV and consider the quality of references supplied.

If you are taking the trouble to interview, you should have established by now that the candidate is basically suitable.

Prepare a list of open-ended questions to ask in the interview. You need to monitor five areas. As you listen to the candidate's replies discreetly award plus or minus marks up to 10 for each quality.

Draw five columns on a sheet of paper and devise questions based on the following notes:

Knowledge and skills	Qualifications and experience	Personal attitude	Personality/calibre	Personal circumstances
Abilities called for?	Educational achievements?	Motivated by money?	For the job?	Age relevant?
Skill to create those abilities?	Proof of potential?	Ambitious for power?	For the team?	Domestic situation?
Skills as starting condition?	Essential experience?	Seeking fame?	Need to lead?	Health and appearance?
Skills picked up on the job?	Desirable experience?	Fired by challenge?	Willing to be led?	Legal considerations? (eg driving license)
Decision making?		Attitude to authority?	What aptitudes?	
Ability to use judgment?		Attitude to subordinates?	A good talker?	
		Attitude to work?	Writer?	
			Staying power?	
			Likely to stay?	

Don't forget to ask yourself:
● Am I abiding by equal opportunity regulations?
● What does intuition tell me about the candidate?

Q

I've been told that I'm a bit abrupt in interviews, but all I try to do is elicit the relevant information without frills or time-wasting. How should I soften my approach?

You can't run an interview as if it were an interrogation. Your role is not simply to establish if the candidate is the right person for the job. You are there to:

● Represent the company to a member of the public.

● Supply information that may influence his/her desire to take the position offered.

It won't do any good to be brusque or to treat prospective staff as if they were part of an assembly line.

The guidelines for effective interviewing are based on common sense:

● One-to-one interviews tend to be more relaxed and productive than panel interviews. Even two people asking questions increases tension and self-consciousness.

● Make clear from the outset the kind of job that's on offer and the special requirements it entails. Describe the workload briefly.

● Don't ask questions as though ticking off points. Avoid those which simply seek a yes or no answer. Candidates will relax more if invited to open up about themselves and their current work. While they're doing so, you can discreetly take notes. Try not to interrupt.

● Don't get too chatty. Remember that there's a job to be filled and try to ascertain, early on, whether the interviewee really wants it or not.

● Ask how candidates see their careers developing and how they would be served by taking on this job. Encourage questions relating to the job, and reply as though you're assuming the candidate will be taking it. A bit of optimism and confidence will make them reveal more about themselves.

Q

Are there any particular danger signs to watch out for in a recruitment interview?

Think twice about offering the job to candidates who:

● Ask about money too early. You'll be dealing with people who care less about the minutiae of the business than the more basic transaction of selling their time.

● Complain about their current or previous boss. Before you know it they'll be complaining about you too.

● Skate over certain stages of their career and won't be drawn to admit what they were doing at the time. Smart candidates are never at a loss about the raffish periods of their past, even if it's the hippy trail to Samarkand. Those who try to conceal such things are lacking maturity.

● Reveal a tendency toward short-stay jobs. It may have been restlessness, or due to insufficient challenge, but it may also have been a chronic condition of unemployability. It's up to you to find out.

● Will not admit to doing anything outside working hours. Do they live only for work? Does it sap all their creative energies? Are they not in danger of becoming a little short of perspective?

Q

One of my best staff has just been 'stolen' by a competitor. Is it legitimate to use similar tactics to replace him?

It's perfectly legitimate to steal staff from competitors. Since you're not dependent for your revenue on their goodwill, where's the harm?

The only grey area, ethically speaking, is in expecting, or requiring, newly poached executives to spill trade, design, financial or marketing secrets about their former company.

The executive search industry exists to find key people in the right jobs and lure them away to a rival concern. Should you decide to employ their services, remember that the inflated sums they will suggest as an appropriate sweetener to the new incumbent will reflect the 10 + per cent commission they will be taking.

Q

I want to apply to a merchant bank. The advertisement asks for hand-written applications only. What's going on?

The company you are seeking to join employs a graphoanalyst – one who assesses personality traits through handwriting.

This comparatively recent and still imperfect science has found considerable favour with banks and similar institutions. Some companies apply it to every job application; others use it only for senior management posts.

Briefly, it means that the way you cross your 't's and dot your 'i's, your Greek 'e's and your elaborate signature, all give away information about your psychological make-up, your emotional life, intelligence, ambitions, confidence, irascibility, tact and many other characteristics that would be hard to detect in an interview.

Anxious scribes may take comfort from the existence, in the US, of 'graphotherapy', which will not only advise you where you're going wrong, but also teach you to write like Lee Iacocca.

Q

The best candidate for the post I advertised is a woman. But she's engaged and in her late twenties, and I'm afraid that she may want to leave and start a family before long. Should I go for a lesser candidate in the hope that he will stay longer?

Sexual discrimination in the business community starts and ends with the manager's fear of a pregnant subordinate who'll leave at the most inappropriate time, return for her maternity benefit, then leave again for a lifetime's motherhood. It's a stereotype and shouldn't prejudice a good manager.

If you think she's the most suitable person, hire her immediately. The best candidate for a job, even if her stay is short, is one who'll bring the right attitude and the right appraising eye to all its operations. That's far more important to the health of the company than employing someone merely because they may stay longer.

Even if she does start a family, nannies, crêches and similar post-natal care services mean that a dedicated executive can be back at work in a matter of weeks. It is a risk, but if she's a valuable team member it's worth taking.

Q

I've been put in charge of an important project and have inherited a team of a dozen people to carry it out. How can I work out the ideal combination of staff talents?

Approach the task as though your staff were a hand of playing cards:

1 Take a card for each member of the team.

2 Write on it a brief resumé of his/her personality traits, skills and rank. Emphasize strengths but record obvious weak points that will have to be covered.

3 Work out the skills the project most needs – creative problem solving, hard graft, etc.

4 Choose a 'middle manager' court card for each specific part of the project. These will form the basis for grouping your people into sub-teams.

5 Assign lower-ranking managers and subordinates to each sub-team so that they:

● Provide support.

● Cover weak points.

● Enable the work to get done.

It is essential that you, as leader, retain an open mind about the combination of skills and talents in your team as a whole and within the sub-groups you create.

Reshuffling the hand to test new combinations should be a priority, rather than an option.

Although ranking as a middle manager, Jack's creative abilities can be maximized by putting him on the same level as 10. His valuable, albeit chaotic, contributions to the project can be harnessed by 10's efficient and orderly approach.

With the analytical King in charge, this

sub-team should be able to take care of the implementation of the project.

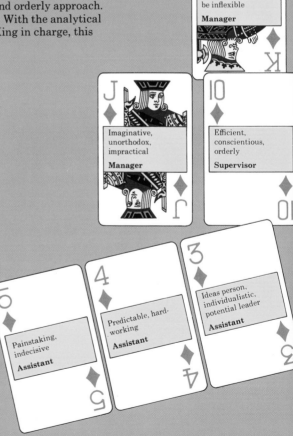

K ◆
Organizer, analytical, tends to be inflexible
Manager

J ◆
Imaginative, unorthodox, impractical
Manager

10 ◆
Efficient, conscientious, orderly
Supervisor

5 ◆
Painstaking, indecisive
Assistant

4 ◆
Predictable, hard-working
Assistant

3 ◆
Ideas person, individualistic, potential leader
Assistant

A ♦

Self confident, in control

Senior Manager
(on the Main Board)

♦

It makes sense to put the Queen in charge of a sub-team where some members need careful handling. The 2 has the personality – calm and well directed – to compensate for 6's weaknesses, but you may have to consider a careful reshuffle if 6 proves to be disruptive. Consider promoting 2 to the same level as 8, 7 and 6 once she has proved she has the ability to carry out the demands and responsibilities of the job.

This sub-team, led by the Queen, should be able to cope with the ideas aspects of the project.

Q ♦

Able, good with people, communicator

Manager

♦

9 ♦

Technically able but introverted

Executive Secretary

♦

8 ♦

Workmanlike but lacks inspiration

Junior Manager

♦

7 ♦

Enthusiastic, communicative, responds to challenge

Junior Manager

♦

6 ♦

Highly strung, impatient, dynamic, good writer

Junior Manager

♦

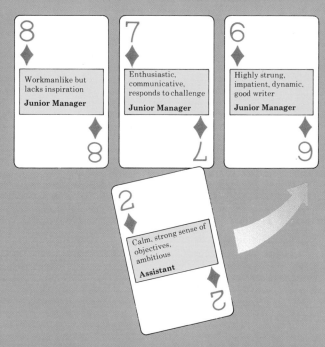

2 ♦

Calm, strong sense of objectives, ambitious

Assistant

♦

Q

I know my staff grumble behind my back because I don't often ask their opinions about the handling of departmental projects. But, as far as I'm concerned, a manager is there to get things done, not to seek the advice of subordinates. Isn't that right?

You are a classic case of the autocratic manager, who delivers the Orders of the Day, assigns work and expects everything to be done as regularly as clockwork.

It's an undemocratic way to behave, but undoubtedly gets things done – provided your judgment is sound. But consider:
● Are you lonely on the exposed heights?
● Would you occasionally like to ask other people if they think anything has been missed out, rather than try to remember it all yourself?
● If three people are reporting to you on three related tasks, might it not be better to discuss with them the best ways of integrating the work?

If you are determined to be a dictator, at least make sure that you:
● Hold regular in-depth progress meetings that give clear instructions.
● Never seem undecided.
● See that instructions filter down, so that everybody's responsibility is clear.

Q

I believe in letting my colleagues have a say in taking decisions. Is there anything wrong with working this way?

Nothing at all, provided it's appropriate to the kind of work you're doing.

Participative, or democratic, management has some attractive features. It:
● Tends to put people before production.
● Takes decisions by popular consensus rather than by diktat.
● Allows subordinates room for creative problem solving.
● Encourages teamwork rather than individual efficiency.
● Takes a liberal approach to work deadlines.

But democratic management is not always the answer. It can:
● Slow down the production process.
● Lead to flaccid compromises between disputatious colleagues, where a definite decision one way or the other would have been more effective.
● Be bad for the morale of people who like being closely supervised, accorded praise or blame and reassured that they are on the right track.

Committee decision making just doesn't carry the same deep, atavistic appeal.

There are certain businesses and company sectors in which management needs to be monolithic and autocratic. Heavy industry, assembly line works, engineering and high-volume retailing are businesses that depend on getting hefty amounts of work done to tight time scales in a strict sequence. There should be as little room as possible for doubt or uncertainty in such organizations. Things should either run like clockwork or not at all.

Likewise, departments into which several downstream processes are being constantly fed cannot afford slip-ups by indecisive line managers.

Remember, the only good thing ever said about dictatorship was that it made the trains run on time.

Q

I've become a senior manager before the age of 30. While I'm pleased at my progress, I don't feel confident about giving orders, especially to my elders. Is there a way to learn to express authority without being dictatorial?

Yes, of course. With many people, your job title should be enough to ensure cooperation. If they're businesslike operators, they'll respond to the hierarchy of rank without the need for you to raise your voice. If you are instinctively aware of where the root of your power lies, you will make others aware of it too.

But sometimes it's as well to be diplomatic about giving orders, especially when you've only just been promoted. This is the time for office politics. You should enlist the help of immediate subordinates, through whom directives can be issued to staff.

If you can remind everyone that you are now in charge, but charm them into acquiescence as well, you are halfway there. Let the heavy hand of authority be seen to come from elsewhere – from supervisors and line managers – while you cultivate the image of paterfamilias and philosopher.

Q

Is it true that leadership cannot be taught?

'Leadership' is a word which defies definition. It's a matter of getting things done by influencing people positively.

Leading people is much more than learning a set of rules. It involves understanding people, knowing what will inspire each one to work harder, appreciating how they will work best as a team, and how they will respond most positively to your presence.

A good leader should cultivate the following skills:

Clarity: people work better if they know exactly what they're doing and how it fits into the larger departmental picture. So:
● Tell them constantly what their targets and objectives are, while letting them know the exact powers and freedom of action they enjoy.

Analytical power: a leader must be a thinker and a visionary, otherwise the individual components of the team's work will become diffused and isolated. Try to:
● See problems before they develop.
● Identify weak links in a communications chain before vital information gets lost.
● Think on your feet and swiftly adapt your team's ground plan to changed circumstances.

Good example: leaders must show what they expect from their people through displaying their own values and beliefs, setting high standards and keeping them:
● Never ask a subordinate to do a job you yourself would not be prepared to do.
● Let people know where they stand and what kind of behaviour they can expect from you.

Gregariousness: since success depends on team performance, a leader must be:
● First among equals – one of the boys (or girls) when necessary, but incontrovertibly in command at other times.
● Approachable, enthusiastic and fair, always ready to listen to opinions and to encourage staff to contribute to discussion.

Compassion: a leader remembers that he or she is dealing with several different people in a team, not a series of behavioural propositions:
● Give priority to the welfare and needs of team members – both psychological and professional.
● Make people feel that they are involved in a worthwhile endeavour which will do them and their careers lasting good.

Q

My company's marketing department has three months in which to launch a new high-profile perfume. How do they manage to get everything done to deadline?

The marketing department works out a project schedule – a flow chart which ties every

	AUGUST			SEPT
MARKET RESEARCH	Receive samples of Exotique and questionnaire for two-week *vox pop* across country by 70 operators under regional supervisor.			Second research sample to compare reactions to Exotique and its competitors
ADVERTISING	Questions for research sample to reach MR dept by Aug 10th.	Receive research results. Creative team to develop ideas.		Copywriter and art director to present campaign to board. Implement refinemen by Sept 21st.
PRESS AND PUBLIC RELATIONS	Press release for consumer press, retail trade, etc. Confirm articles in fashion magazines and colour supplements to tie-in with launch.	Contact trade press for 'premature leaks' about appeal of new perfume.		Lunch with beauty editors of major women's magazines.
DESIGN	Finalize design of perfume bottle.	Liaise with Advertising on designs for packaging and promo material.		Design of box and logo to be show to the board by Sept 11th.
SALES		Sales director to brief regional team. Seven key areas of country. SD to promote perfume and ask team to name best outlets.		Regional managers to identi 10 retailers for special prom Samples ready for inspection from Production.
ADMINISTRATION	Special forms required to monitor market research.	Credit terms for suppliers to be finalized.		Collation of MR findings. Results to Advertising.
LAUNCH PARTY	Book function room at Casterbridge Hotel.	Accept tenders for catering. Decide in seven days.		Discuss special function effects with party planning consultant.

task to a date. 'Liaisons' are indicated so that individuals do not work in isolation. Work is evenly distributed between sections.

The initial market gap research has been conducted and the perfume is under production. The flow chart looks like this:

...MBER ➝	←	OCTOBER	➝	
	Third research sample to assess public reaction to advertising (shown to passers-by) and report findings.			
	Receive schedule of TV commercials and full-page colour ads in women's magazines.		Eve-of-launch teaser ads in press and train stations.	
	Liaise with launch coordinators re replies from press.		Send out press release on launch.	**DEADLINE NOVEMBER 1st**
Feed diary items to newspapers on aphrodisiacal qualities of Exotique.		Suggest profile of MD to newspaper columnists.		
Four-colour printing from Mondovongole, Italy, to be completed by Oct 5th.			Provide point-of-sale material for sales promotion in up-market department stores.	
Sales director to monitor team's progress in provinces. Negotiate incentive discounts with board. Liaison with Advertising.			Send Sales reps all over country.	
Special pro-forma invoices for sales outlets partaking in special promo.		Reps' samples and mobile stock – new checking system to be devised for rapid quality and quantity control.		
Paraphernalia – hire screens, trestle tables, microphones.	Send out invitations and open file to list accepters and no-shows.	All speeches to have been written and approved. Book transport for VIPs.	Liaise with PR re numbers attending.	

Q

I have a mountain of work for which I am responsible. How can I possibly get other people to do some of it for me without losing control?

To be a manager, you must think like a manager.

'I have a mountain of work' should be translated as 'there is a great deal of work to be performed by my department, under my instruction and implementation'.

Delegation is the heart of the management game, and learning to delegate tasks to the most appropriate people is its central skill.

There should be a clear distinction in your mind between assigning tasks (saying 'Do this') and delegating work (saying 'I want you to apply yourself to this problem'). Make sure your subordinates are made to feel:

● They have been given responsibility, rather than merely work.
● The problem is solvable by teamwork, of which they are a necessary part.
● Their suggestions will be of some value.

With apt delegation, the problem of 'control' should not arise.

Giving staff clear instructions and information deadlines means you will be kept supplied with constant inputs of work for you to correlate.

Delegation should be seen as the enlightened sharing of work around a department of variegated but valuable talents, in a way that:

● Extends the boundaries of people's natural capacities.
● Raises morale.
● Ensures that staff are being made proper use of.
● Leaves the manager to assess the department's work output with detachment.

Assigning tasks

'Look up these sales figures and check them against last year's, and let me have the percentage difference by lunchtime.'

The subordinate's reaction:
● 'I'm no more than a piece of processing equipment.'
● 'There's no need for me to think about why this task has to be accomplished.'

Leads to:
● Resentment.
● Disaffection.
● Perfunctory work.

Delegating work

'The board can't understand why we seem to be selling more of Brand X in Cambridge than in Manchester. They want to look at the whole sales operation nationwide and see how it compares with last year. Could you look at the figures and have a think about how we can evaluate them?'

The subordinate's reaction:
● 'To solve this problem I need to use my initiative.'
● 'To be given this responsibility must mean that I'm a valued member of the team.'

Leads to:
● Increased commitment.
● Personal enthusiasm.
● The likelihood of a more imaginative approach

Q

I gave a subordinate a task which he carried out poorly. Should I give him easier assignments or take back the work and do it myself?

Delegation that produces poor results is more often due to managerial misjudgment than executive inefficiency. It means you haven't identified sufficiently accurately the various strengths, work traits and personal preferences of the staff under your command.

Giving an organizational conundrum to a diffident bureaucrat will obviously get you nowhere. But giving a mundane task to a creative high-flyer is just as bad.

There's no substitute for instinct in this area of management – but some theorists enjoin the making of employee 'charts' on which marks out of 10 are awarded for:
1 Communication skills, both verbal and written.
2 Speed and accuracy of dispatch, track record of throughput to a deadline.
3 Organizational qualities, tidiness of both desk and disposition.
4 Creative strength, ability to see beyond foreground details.
5 Degree of perfectionism, and its half-brother, nit-picking.

An executive who scores low in one of these sections may, nevertheless, be suited to a job that requires specific skills: the detail-obsessed and the creatively flamboyant both have their parts to play. It's a matter of finding the right person for the right job.

And no, of course you don't do the work yourself. That way lies madness, ulcers, alcoholism and ruined weekends. Think about it: if you were habitually to re-do or take on board the tasks delegated to all your subordinates, two things would happen:
● They would give up trying (since anything they did would be liable to be blue-pencilled by you).
● You would become responsible for everything that happened in the office and would never be able to leave it.

Q

I have delegated to my assistant some important research work which I need to ensure is correct and on time. How should I monitor her progress?

Trust your assistant to find her own level of work efficiency. Although you must be ready to correct her mistakes and to understand her approach to problems, don't expect her to work in the same way as you.

It's crucial that you clarify what's expected of her before you start monitoring her performance:
1 Precisely what results do you require?
2 By what date do you want to see such results?
3 If decisions need to be taken in order to complete the work, how much authority will she be able to invoke?
4 What operating budget should she work with?
5 Will interim reports be expected and to whom should they be submitted?
6 Are there related areas of enquiry that she should avoid?

Apart from these considerations, ask only to be kept informed of any deadline problems.

Q

I'm a conscientious worker, but I can't seem to get myself noticed when important positions fall vacant. What gets you promoted, and what actively hinders progress?

Being conscientious isn't enough. It's essential to project an air of 'added value', of initiative, style and flair.

Achieve this by displaying your innate energy and confidence, by learning appropriate skills and, to some extent, by acting the part.

It isn't necessary to pull off spectacular managerial coups; just to emphasize your most positive qualities, to think beyond the immediate perimeters of the job and to keep a sharp eye on gaps in the hierarchy.

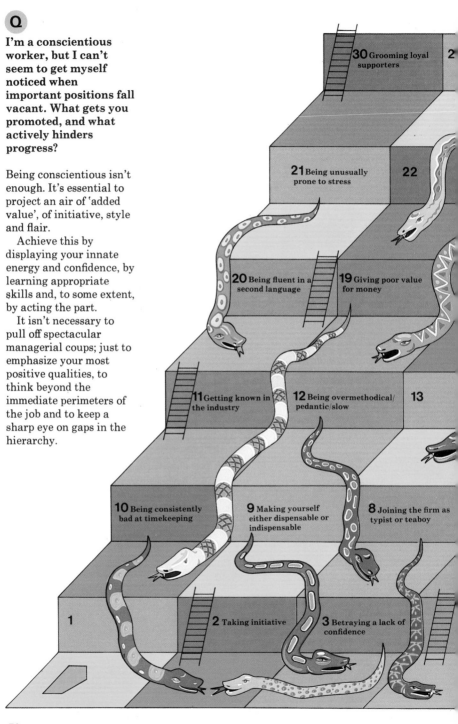

30 Grooming loyal supporters

2

21 Being unusually prone to stress

22

20 Being fluent in a second language

19 Giving poor value for money

11 Getting known in the industry

12 Being overmethodical/ pedantic/slow

13

10 Being consistently bad at timekeeping

9 Making yourself either dispensable or indispensable

8 Joining the firm as typist or teaboy

1

2 Taking initiative

3 Betraying a lack of confidence

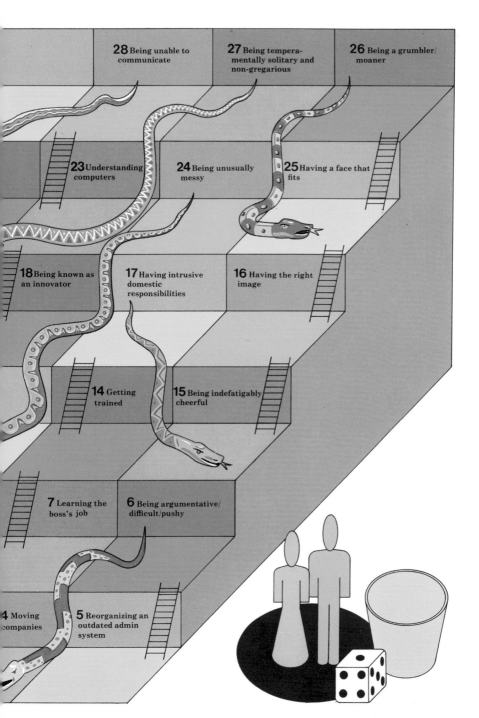

28 Being unable to communicate

27 Being temperamentally solitary and non-gregarious

26 Being a grumbler/moaner

23 Understanding computers

24 Being unusually messy

25 Having a face that fits

18 Being known as an innovator

17 Having intrusive domestic responsibilities

16 Having the right image

14 Getting trained

15 Being indefatigably cheerful

7 Learning the boss's job

6 Being argumentative/difficult/pushy

4 Moving companies

5 Reorganizing an outdated admin system

Q

I have five talented junior managers all of whom should be considered for a senior vacancy. How do I choose?

Although talented, are all the managers equally keen to be promoted? Plenty of supervisors and junior overseers are content to stay put and to defer taking on extra responsibility.

Don't promote someone just because you think that he or she:
● Deserves recognition.
● May otherwise leave the firm.
● Is a troublemaker who won't complain if pushed upstairs.

The vacancy must suit one manager better than another – it must require certain skills, talents or training:
● Analyze the special skills required in the senior job.
● Ask yourself to what extent you can see each candidate in turn as a leader, an accepter of responsibility, and an efficient supervisor of other people's work.

You should also be looking for:
● Above-average work output, indicating untapped capacity.
● Willingness to exceed their quota.
● Those who, with training, would be motivated beyond their peers.

Q

What characterizes management development (as opposed to training) programmes?

Management training programmes are designed to improve the abilities of all the company's management. They anticipate the future of the company, and seek to adapt to new ways, organizational methods and technical requirements.

Management development programmes, on the other hand, offer special assistance to promising managers or unusually qualified specialists. These people aren't just trained into new jobs – they are given the opportunity to take the company into whole new areas.

The aim of development programmes is to:
● Provide an appropriate base of properly qualified, flexible and omnicompetent executives to ensure the company's survival.
● Anticipate succession. As the company changes, grows, diversifies or specializes, it will need top-quality people within its ranks.

Development programmes exist in various forms:
1 Academic programmes: some companies favour a 'sandwich course', in which a new recruit's university education is paid for by the company, provided he or she has worked for them for a certain time.

Extracurricular degrees (Open University, night classes, extramural or correspondence diplomas) should be encouraged. A company shouldn't necessarily offer financial help for the course, but should recognize that a new competence increases staff members' worth, both to the company and in terms of salary on the open market.

2 Specialist programmes: aspiring managers may be sent by their companies to be taught specific skills beyond the current reach or competence of the company. These may include a study of exporting or computers.

3 General programmes: of perhaps the most value to the modern company is the trained generalist. Rather than becoming a middle-management expert, the generalist is groomed for the top.

He or she is given a wide-ranging induction into the broad industrial scene, the sociology and psychology of industry – everything, in short, that would enable a future board member to display knowledge, wisdom and a broad frame of reference when discoursing with colleagues.

Developing skills 42–5 *Teams and groups* 62–5

Q

My best resources are my people. They are all intelligent and hardworking. How can I develop their talents even further?

Start by asking your staff which aspects of their jobs they like best and least and what they'd like to be doing that they're not doing now.

Job rotation is a well-proven way of keeping all the staff interested while training them in general management by providing an overview of the company.

The PEOPLexpress Airline conducts a successful policy of 'horizontal management', in which, broadly speaking, everyone does everyone else's job: the majority of staff are known as 'Customer Services Managers' and swap roles every month.

If your management trainees show promise, consider putting them to work as assistants to the senior managers. This will give them invaluable experience 'at the sharp end'. The injection of youthful brilliance should enhance, rather than disrupt, the organizational style at the top.

Q

Should I send middle managers on external training courses or should I coach them 'on the job'?

The type of training you choose depends on what you expect your staff to gain from it.

1 'Learning by doing', consists of showing your middle managers how to do something, then watching until he or she performs it correctly.

It may be crude, but on the job training is the most effective method of teaching task-related skills and the only way to teach staff how to process unfamiliar forms or how to use new technology.

2 Internal training programmes run by your company's training section will naturally reflect the particular needs of your business and are thus more valuable than the courses offered by external organizations.

3 Training programmes run by management centres are designed to teach specific disciplines, such as basic computer studies, finance, marketing strategy, project management and foreign languages.

The British Management Training Development Council publishes up-to-date lists of the training programmes run by management centres, institutes and societies, most of them to diploma or degree level.

Before sending managers away, you must decide whether you can afford to lose valued members of staff for comparatively long periods. Certainly they will be grateful for the boost their new knowledge will give them – but your short-term operations might be badly affected.

4 Psychological training methods often involve a group, in the midst of which an executive is encouraged to act out a 'real life' drama – usually a confrontation which demands quick thinking under pressure. The whole team is encouraged to supply comments and criticisms.

Staff who need to be expert at dealing quickly with delicate situations may benefit from this type of training.

5 'Sensitivity training' sessions, in which executives are encouraged to come to terms with their responses and feelings toward each other, are of limited value and you should be wary of them.

Courses which provide the executive with the chance to indulge in full-scale war games with platoons, toy bombs and make-believe mayhem are an expensive way to ring the changes.

Q

Why is my company losing key staff?

A high turnover of staff is a symptom of poor senior management. One of the qualitative judgments made on a company is its record of keeping people.

First, you must look at your company's recruitment procedures. Perhaps employees who leave were bad risks. Perhaps they turned out to lack know-how, to be poorly motivated from the outset or to be short on personal qualities that would fit the company's 'culture'. In that case you'll have to make sure that interview techniques are improved.

ARE KEY STAFF LEAVING FOR SIMILAR JOBS?

YES   NO

Low earnings lead to dissatisfaction. If pay is bad, staff won't stay long. NO

Does the company operate a fair system of wage and salary reviews? YES

YES

Are staff leaving for higher salaries? NO

NO

Are staff leaving for increased status? NO

Are they seeking better career prospects? YES

YES

Social/professional kudos can be a potent motivator.

Comfortable, congenial working conditions are basic needs.

YES

Recognition stirs people to achieve more and to stay.

Are working conditions likely to be creating dissatisfaction? NO

YES

Is management uncommunicative, unappreciative of people's efforts? NO

Has the company put extra strain on staff, eg overtime demands? YES

Recruitment **58–61**   *Teams and groups* **62–5**

If you are confident that staff are well selected for their qualifications, strengths, personal drive and impact on others, you must establish what has gone wrong since they joined your company. It could be management style or conditions of work.

Above all, management must understand staff's motivation needs and make sure, as far as possible, that they are met.

Try to analyze your personnel failings by asking:

Money is a basic motivating factor. Risk giving slightly too much, a little too early.

Safety is a basic human need. Review policy on health and safety, retirement, sickness and redundancy.

YES

Interesting and challenging work are important motivators

Are they going for jobs with more responsibility?

NO Are they going for more security?

YES

YES

Responsibility and achievement are important to skilled employees.

NO Are they going for more assistants?

NO Are they going for more stimulating/challenging jobs?

Advancement is a key motivator in keeping skilled staff.

YES

NO

Are they status seekers? Is there room for them? Do they deserve it?

NO Has the job genuinely grown?

Let them go, unless there's another reason for their departure.

YES

YES

A supportive, caring environment is a basic need. Provide extra help and/or technology.

If tension and stress are the cause try to remove it. Encourage staff to see the doctor.

YES

NO

Is the strain temporary?

NO Caused by overwork?

YES Apply principles of time management, employ more staff.

Q

As far as I can see, the only true motivator is money. What other kinds can there be in business?

Simple financial reward isn't enough to get people working better, let alone at their best. But then no one tangible item is sufficient: not a perfect office, nor a considerate boss, nor a cheap staff canteen, nor even a share in the profits. People's requirements are more subtle than that.

An important initial distinction should be made between motivation and satisfaction. The latter is more easily achieved but is a form of complacency that has little to do with striving. In Peter Drucker's view, it's a problem of history.

'The present concern with satisfaction arose out of the realization that fear no longer supplies the motivation for the worker in industrial society. But instead of facing the problem created by the disappearance of fear as the motive, the concern with satisfaction sidesteps it.

'What we need is to replace the externally imposed spur of fear with an internal self-motivation for performance. Responsibility – not satisfaction – is the only thing that will serve.'

The most commonly accepted non-financial motivators are:

● Responsibility and achievement. These provide the job's own motivation. A sense of 'personal best', of individual effort, provides its own reward.
● Social/professional kudos. The young executive's desire for recognition prompts him/her to seek difficult or high-profile work to get noticed.
● Intrinsic interest in the work. A systems analyst with a passion for large computers will work harder if there is a goal in sight where he/she can indulge such an interest.
● The reward system. This incentive encourages concentrated work.
● Influence of others. Many people work unusually hard for bosses who can offer no apparent reward other than their approbation.
● A congenial working environment. Poor working conditions, unsatisfactory terms of employment and a tyrannical management are de-motivating factors, particularly when coupled with insufficient remuneration. However, an improvement in a single area wouldn't necessarily help.

Q

A number of my staff work at a glorified assembly line, testing microchip circuits. I know it's rather uninspiring work, but I need to keep them. I can't afford to pay them more or change their titles. How can I motivate them?

People who only process other people's work can get terribly bored. Do their responsibilites have to end with simply checking the circuits? Is there nothing useful they could do at the next stage of assembly?

Why not consider making them an autonomous department, charged with supplying fully-checked, mounted and suitably cased microchip circuit boards to be fitted, entire, into the company's products? They'll be much happier working to create a product they can see before them.

Should that be impractical, try changing their hours. Think of the job as a matter of quota management and tell your assemblers that their working time is immaterial provided they supply a certain number of tested items per day. This is a classic case of the reward system, offering extra leisure time.

Q

Is it possible to keep my staff happy, hard-working and ambitious?

That's precisely where motivation comes in. You must inspire them with the will to do better, and the drive to further the company's interests – but to do so voluntarily, as part of a larger concept of self-interest.

● Find out what they want from their jobs and use the information. Gerry wants to run General Motors some day? Encourage him in decision-making roles, show him what delegation involves, act as though everything you're giving him to do is a dry run for future stardom. You're putting his natural inclinations to good use.

● Find out about their extra-business ambitions. If Kelly's a demon golfer, make her think of the productivity bonus that might pay for a golfing holiday.

● Always think of your staff in terms of 'what's next?' Don't be content with what they can do already. Give them opportunities they seek – provided they're ready to take them.

If they're being held back by weakness in one area, help them and make sure they realize you have their interests at heart in doing so.

● Appreciation is a potent motivator. Don't be too lavish with praise, but do recognize good work – and let the other staff and your superiors know about it too. You should make it clear to your subordinates what will win them credits or debits.

● Make people think for themselves. Ask their opinions, share information and encourage them to join you in thinking around a problem.

● Delegate liberally to those whom you feel would like to take on more work. Don't keep the most interesting or creative tasks for yourself.

● Explore some of the wide range of incentive schemes now available. In many of these, a simple points system runs up credits for members of staff, until they can be cashed in for prizes. They're popular, very 'visible' and obviously attuned to rewarding effort.

Q

The staff in the department I've taken over are slack and inefficient, although they are well paid and have interesting jobs. Could working conditions be the cause?

Inefficiency and absenteeism may well be caused by adverse working conditions. Are your employees:

● Crowded uncomfortably together?

● Facing directly into a light source?

● Expected to spend several hours a day seated in one position?

● Subjected to excessive noise?

● Too hot or too cold?

● Unable to move around without having to squeeze past some obstacle?

● Seated so far from others with related job functions as to make *ad hoc* consultations impossible?

● Close to others who smoke, talk incessantly or have other distracting habits?

Ask your staff for suggestions as to how the office could be improved. You'll be surprised how many grudges will surface.

Delegation **68–9** *Decision making* **82–5** *Working conditions* **98–9**   77

Q

Our company encourages managers to give staff annual performance reviews. Is there a better way of telling them what I think of their work?

Once a year is not enough. Too much will have happened between appraisals for them to be adequate reflections of work done. If people like to be told how they are doing, and what their prospects are, you should let them know constantly.

The best method of continuous appraisal is the encouraging of greater cooperation between management and individual employees. Once the staff become used to a flow of reaction and response they may feel emboldened to comment constructively on your own behaviour and approach.

There is no need to set up elaborate procedures for continuous assessment. Just allocate extra time for studying the work of individuals, discussing it with them, and sorting out problems, encouraging initiative and setting new goals.

Q

I make a point of encouraging my staff in their work, pointing out particularly fine day-to-day achievements. Yet instead of being motivated they don't seem to try harder. Are they simply ungrateful?

No. The problem lies in your well-intentioned reactions to their work.

If you constantly gush praise on your staff they will soon start to wonder when to expect some concrete rewards such as promotions or pay rises. They will worry if you start speaking in anything less than superlatives, and you will be caught in a trap of your own making.

The staff who don't try harder have learned that your praise doesn't have any substance. So temper your exuberance and refrain from making extravagant promises of advancement unless you can back them up at board level.

Try instead to criticize or praise individual details, rather than overall performance. Then you will find yourself congratulating a correct procedure rather than an individual.

Q

How should I conclude an appraisal? With a pat on the back, with parental advice or with specific directives about details of work?

Appraisals are a waste of time and effort unless some form of counselling results from them. An appraisal should not be thought of as (a) the employee telling the manager how he/she is doing, followed by (b) the manager dispensing wisdom.

An appraisal must be worked through together by appraiser and appraised.

Before you can really discuss and evaluate performance, you must decide on the results that you, as a manager, expect to see, and these goals must be agreed on. It is always advisable to have something definable and/or measurable to appraise.

Appraisals should end in mutual agreement. Finish by setting a date by which certain results should be evident.

Q

What sort of questions should I ask at staff appraisals, and what should I expect the appraisal to achieve?

What you get from an appraisal depends on what you put into it.

As a rule, the questions you ask should be those that lead to the most detailed discussion, and that keep the convergence of the person and the job firmly in sight.

If properly handled, appraisals can provide a wide variety of information, help you set targets and reveal problem areas hitherto unsuspected.

INPUT   Questions to ask

What do you think you are particularly good at?

What are your weakest points?

What are the most difficult problems you have had to face in the past six months?

Who (confidentially) do you find it difficult to work with?

Are there any parts of the office procedure you consider to be in need of a radical overhaul?

Which part of your job interests you most?

How do you see your future within the company?

How do you see your future in the department?

Is there anything/anyone you need in order to develop your job and become more effective?

Why did the project under your care fail to deliver on time/run massively over budget?

Where is the weak point in your communication chain?

Is there anything in your job description that has become redundant or you would wish to change?

Are you happy?

OUTPUT   Information, targets   and achievements

Executives' progress over the last six months/year is reviewed.

Feelings of motivation are refreshed.

A halt is put to lingering, unresolved problems.

Personal conflicts are identified/resolved.

Job descriptions are scrutinized and updated.

Information is provided for salary and promotion reviews.

Ambitious new targets, agreed between appraiser and appraised, are set.

Staff are encouraged to examine their own work more closely.

Executives are made to feel that their efforts have been noticed and will probably be rewarded.

Q

What constitutes unacceptable behaviour and thus counts as a sacking offence?

The most obvious are:
● Violent or abusive behaviour.
● Drunken incapacity.
● Drug taking.
● Gross moral turpitude.
● Stealing.
● Embezzlement.
● Malicious representation, libel or slander.
● Wilful destruction of company property.

Less clear cut is the area of non-cooperation. Many good executives develop unreasoning hatreds of new staff members and refuse to work with them. Such personality clashes may defeat logic, but must be firmly handled. You must point out that the job must come first, and that personal prejudices are far down the priority line.

People who bring the company into disrepute, by inappropriate extra-curricular activities (especially of a political nature) are a burden you can do without.

Hot-tempered managers who engage subordinates in corridor rows or spread unwelcome gossip should be taken to one side and told to stop.

When personality is the problem rather than performance, a little direct advice carries more weight than the threat of dismissal.

Q

I reprimand my staff as and when the occasion arises. I believe in instant praise or blame and like everyone to know where they stand at all times, and what I will not tolerate. So why do they persist in flouting the rules?

Probably because you're such a tactless bully. You're not on the parade ground, you're in the world of business where certain subtleties operate. It is time that you learned them.

There are four essentials to remember about reprimands:
1 Never reprimand staff in public – that's the place for praise only. Deal with reprimands on a one-to-one basis.
2 Do not talk in terms of 'blame' or think of mistakes as being someone's 'fault'. The reasons why someone took a certain course of action are complex. It is your responsibility to locate the fractured logic that lay behind an unwise decision so that others may not fall victim to the same accident.
3 The notion of instant praise or blame is an unhealthy one for any manager to entertain. It's the quickest way to turn staff into neurotic 'yes-people'. A good manager should have time to reflect on the facts and react to them with due consideration.
4 People may know where you stand, but they won't necessarily agree with you.

There is a far more pleasant and effective approach to reprimand and discipline. When you have all the facts relating to a mistake, see if you can locate the reason for it. Ask yourself questions such as these:
● Has the transgressor done something similar before?
● Were your instructions clear?
● Was the failure technological in origin?
● Was it all due to a small but significant misunderstanding?
● Was it due to lack of ability?
● Was more training or experience needed?
● Was the person under stress?
● What *happened* to them?

On a personal basis, call the wrongdoer to see you in private and explain clearly what has gone wrong. Make sure the person recognizes how the mistake was made. End the conversation with a line such as 'So if you could watch that in future . . .', but be aware of the need for better briefing, more training and other back-ups you can provide.

Establish, above all, trust and understanding, so that the job will be done correctly next time.

Q

I have to fire two of my staff because they have failed to come up to expectations. How do I go about it?

Firing staff is an aspect of their jobs that managers relish least. It's a delicate but unlovely operation in which three basic rules should be observed:

1 Keep it factual.
2 Make it fair.
3 Do it with speed but not haste.

Legally, you can't fire someone merely because they have 'failed to come up to expectations'. You must have a clear set of written rules, if necessary drawn up in collaboration with the union, covering both dismissal and redundancy.

In such an agreement, terms must be set out for any financial compensation. Each employee should have a contract in which their job description is clearly stated, plus any sackable offences particular to the company, such as working for close rivals.

You can fire people for:
● Consistently failing to perform certain duties clearly laid down in their job description.
● Constantly arriving late and/or leaving early.
● Sloppy work.
● Disruption of other members of staff through rows and confrontations.
● Refusal to apply themselves.

In firing someone, you can give any of these reasons, but only provided you have first given the defaulters verbal, then written warnings that their work must improve in certain aspects or they will face dismissal.

Disciplinary chats should always be conducted in private. Invite the miscreant into your office and explain exactly how he or she is:
● Reflecting badly on the company.
● Interrupting or delaying the production process by inefficiency, idleness or forgetfulness.
● Disrupting the office atmosphere by causing friction.
● Displaying signs of carelessness.
● Appearing to be unmotivated or uninterested.
● Failing to produce work of a specified standard.

Keep such an interview as objective as possible. Address yourself, as far as you can, to the problem rather than the person. Conclude by asking for an undertaking that things will actively change for the better, not just cease to go wrong, and set a realistic date for a reassessment.

If, by your specified date, no improvement is forthcoming, write a coolly factual letter stating precisely what the problem has been in the past and your reasons for believing that it remains unimproved.

Call in the person for a second meeting (which should be kept as friendly as circumstances will allow, though a certain chill will be inevitable) and hand over the letter. Make sure it is understood that failure to improve will result in dismissal. Again, give a date by which you will make a final assessment. If there is no alternative to firing staff, be brisk but correct.

Consult the Personnel department and make sure you are not in breach of any legal agreement.

Inform the remaining staff as soon as possible, and be as reassuring and informal as you can. Rumours and gossip will proliferate soon enough about the reasons for the dismissal.

Finally, be prepared to cope with resentments and reprisals over your action.

Q

Which comes first when company decisions have to be made – money or people?

Neither. Every decision made is a conscious synthesis of three distinct responsibilities: work, people and resources. A decision seeks to reconcile conflicts between them. There may be:

● More than one resource at stake (say, money and computer time).

● Conflicts with other areas of the organization (between, say, the admin office and sales).

● Short-term benefits that need weighing against long-term growth.

Smart managers resolve these warring elements, while remembering their main responsibilites:

● Making things happen.

● Getting effective performance.

● Getting value for money.

People decision

You would like to promote a member of staff. Your decision is influenced by:

● Finance: what promotion will cost.

● Work: how promotion will affect the balance and delegation of work.

● People: how other members of staff will react. The danger of breeding resentment. The problems of finding a replacement.

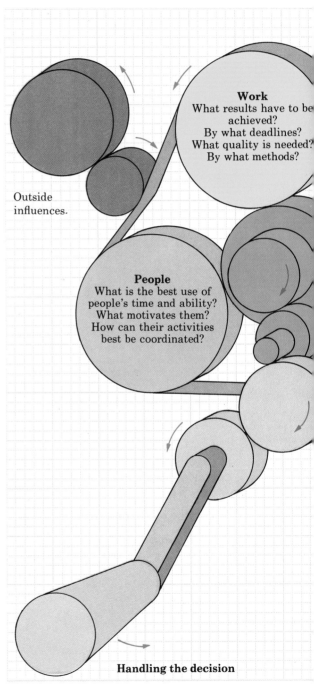

Outside influences.

Work
What results have to be achieved?
By what deadlines?
What quality is needed?
By what methods?

People
What is the best use of people's time and ability?
What motivates them?
How can their activities best be coordinated?

Handling the decision

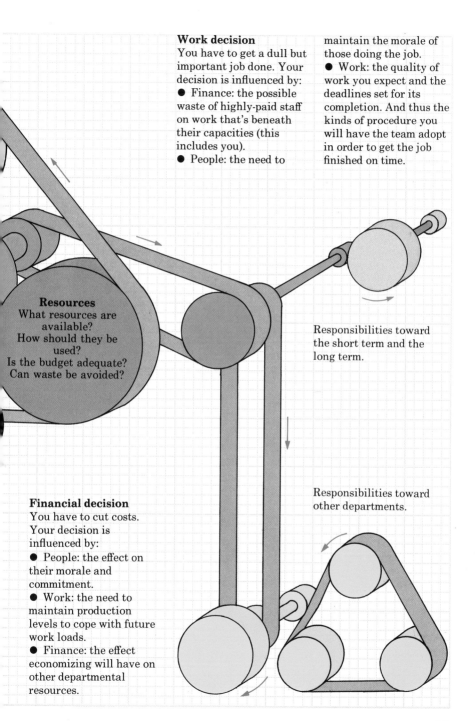

Work decision
You have to get a dull but important job done. Your decision is influenced by:
● Finance: the possible waste of highly-paid staff on work that's beneath their capacities (this includes you).
● People: the need to maintain the morale of those doing the job.
● Work: the quality of work you expect and the deadlines set for its completion. And thus the kinds of procedure you will have the team adopt in order to get the job finished on time.

Resources
What resources are available?
How should they be used?
Is the budget adequate?
Can waste be avoided?

Responsibilities toward the short term and the long term.

Responsibilities toward other departments.

Financial decision
You have to cut costs. Your decision is influenced by:
● People: the effect on their morale and commitment.
● Work: the need to maintain production levels to cope with future work loads.
● Finance: the effect economizing will have on other departmental resources.

Q

I have been criticized for taking decisions based on instinct. But my gut reaction has been proved right time and time again. Must decisions be based on logic alone?

Certainly not. Logic based on false assumptions can lead to terrible trouble. Gut reaction, however, is a far from reliable alternative. Your ill-defined, emotional promptings may have been 'proved right' in the past, but why discard objectivity?

The way to approach decision making is by weighing up evidence and examining options with a calm, objective mind.

In business decision making there's rarely a single best-case option, let alone one that is so obvious that it can be detected by logic or grasped by instinct.

Of several possible alternatives, only a few will be genuinely practicable for the unique problem under examination. One will be safe, one over-cautious, one bold, one foolhardy, one brilliant but risky, one disastrous.

Identify the options by matching the action to the proposed outcome. Don't risk the embarrassment of having to say later, 'I don't know why I did – I've always been right before.'

Q

I can make snap decisions about comparatively minor things but sometimes feel overwhelmed by pros and cons when faced with larger, departmental issues. How can I be sure to take the right decision every time?

You can't. There is no such thing. Decisions aren't 'right' or 'wrong'; they are good, bad, effective, compromised, adequate, controversial or any number of other provisional adjectives.

A decision may be 'wise' – but that isn't to say that a wiser one cannot be found. Your aim should be to have enough information to reach, at least, a workable decision.

You can decide what to do about small issues because their outcome won't materially affect the company's health, or because they're matters of taste. Nonetheless, it's important that you notice there's a process of choice implicit in the simplest decisions – even presenting a report to your boss tacitly suggests that you approve it. Arranging a meeting – making something happen – implies an active decision.

Scaling down all those pros and cons that so confuse you is the only way to become more proficient at the art of making up you mind. Strive to arrive at the point at which the options are reduced to two:

1 Define your objective(s).
2 Establish an order of importance if there is more than one.
3 Make sure you have all the facts or, if not, you know where to get them.
4 Seek parallel problems or experiences in other departments or companies if you can.
5 Ask the relevant institute or trade association for a ruling if you think it will help.
6 Make an exhaustive list of options available.
7 Ask again what outcome you envisage and specify two possible courses of action. Of course there will be others, but go for just two to begin with. Any more than that and you'll find yourself lost in a phenomenological fog.
8 Pick one course of action and act on it.

If your researches yield two possibilities that are indistinguishable – or that you genuinely cannot decide between – close your eyes and stick a pin in one. Then defend your choice with vehemence.

Once you've taken a decision, you're entitled to change your mind should a new suggestion be put forward.

Q

I delegate work in my department but make sure subordinates consult me about final procedure. The problem is that I'm constantly interrupted by their queries. What can I do?

Re-think your approach to delegating and decision making.

Good managers, while remaining responsible for everything they delegate, make as few decisions as possible. They concentrate on those that will cost the company a great deal of money and represent many people's time and expertise. They leave lesser matters to decision-makers down the management line.

However much you may dislike being responsible for decisions taken by subordinates, you should recognize that people directly confronted by the problems are better placed than you to judge the practical results.

By delegating routine management tasks to your staff, without allowing them to make policy decisions, you're stifling their creativity. Release them from your autocratic grip and they'll be twice as effective; and you'll be freed to devote yourself to the 'generic' decisions a serious executive should be taking.

Q

I'm always suspicious when people respond to my decisions with 'OK – consider it done'. I go out of my way to check they're doing what I want. Am I being unduly tenacious?

Not at all. Decisions without implementation are no more than happy thoughts or bright ideas. And too many people confuse the intention with the act.

You're quite right to ensure your wishes are carried out; a manager's authority includes the right to have his/her decisions acted on.

When you've decided on a course of action, delegate it immediately:
● Choose somebody capable of taking charge, who will be solely and directly answerable to you.
● Tell the staff and bosses who will be affected.
● Brief the staff as a group; miss nobody out.
● Follow the briefing with written statements itemizing every stage of the proposed action.
● Devise a checking system to assess how precisely your instructions are being carried out.

Once you're dealing in deadlines rather than promises, you may leave it to your subordinate, trusting that he/she will come to you with any difficulties.

Q

In a crisis, is it important to make a decision, even if it's the wrong one?

Yes, it is. An unresolved crisis will deteriorate rapidly, while you and your colleagues dither and worry. Making a decision one way or the other must be a better move – even if it precipitates further problems.

First, however, make sure that you are the right person to take this decision. It's vital that you are aware of the limits of your responsibility.

If you notice a fault on the production line, and decide instantly to abort the whole process, you might save the company money. But if you take it on yourself to ignore some contractual stipulation because you think it may not be legal, take care you are not exceeding your authority. Even if your decision is deemed good and right, you may get a reprimand.

Initiative should always be rewarded. Positive decision making, whatever the outcome, will always be encouraged. Taking decisions above your station, however, will not win much approval.

Role and position **22–3** *Delegation* **68–9** *Conflict and crisis* **88–9**

Q

I enjoy haggling over money but often come off worst because of the tricks employed by my opponents. How can I learn to negotiate more effectively?

Use a combination of strategy and tactics:

1 Leave it to the other side to make the first mention of money.
2 Refer to the competition as though they, rather than your opponent's company, represent the market *status quo*.
3 Implying you don't need all the functions and services included in a sales package isn't strictly relevant but it confuses the issue and makes a lower price seem justified.
4 Beware using round numbers – they're too negotiable.
5 Both the price and the intrinsic value of the package may be talked up or down at any time but not, generally, together. Sellers should expand the value while holding the price. Unless the other party brings in the piggy-back play.
6 The piggyback play. Any speculative raising of the buyer's price will call for additional extras, sweeteners, perks and bonuses.

● Be thoroughly briefed about the subject.
● Marshal the available facts to use as ammunition in your discussion.
● Arm yourself with both an ideal and a realistic 'bottom line' figure to settle on.

● Have notes handy to remind yourself of fresh arguments and counter-arguments.
● Make sure you have the budget allocation (and therefore the figure you'll settle for) burned on your brain, and that your initial monetary

---

Negotiator A I'm glad to hear you were impressed with the specifications. The manufacturers' recommended price is £50,000. ❶ **£50,000**

    Negotiator B *That's laughably high for this kind of machine, as far as I can see. It's no different in essence from the Yakitori 900 Series. They're going for £28,000, and so, realistically, should this.* ❷

But they're quite different computers. The Pomegranate's memory is twice as large as the Yakitori's, it has a multi-user facility, and can be linked to Textline Services.

    That's all very well, but we don't really need such a large ❸ *memory – our invoicing and sales records are all handled by the big IBM mainframe. We want this more for the financial modelling software.*

There's no better . . .

    And if we took it, we'd be looking at – well the Yakitori **£30,000** *has, if I may say so, a rather bigger reputation – £26,500* ❹ *would be about right.*

I wish I could help you, but I'm afraid the price stays the same. Perhaps I should have pointed out that it **£45,000** includes delivery, installation and warranty. ❺

    So do most prices.

And since you're a valued customer, there's a discount available for an early order.

    Hmmm. We might consider £30,000, were you prepared to ❻ **£32,000** *supply floppy disks and to phase in the new daisywheel printer.*

I'm sorry, but the printer isn't properly in production yet, so we have no pricing structure for it.

    But surely for an old and valued customer . . .

I'm sorry Chris, it's not negotiable. The floppy disks on ❼ the other hand, we could let you have in discount bulk to show our goodwill. But the machine itself is **£40,000** available only at the MRP less discount. Unless, of course, you were prepared to help us out in a small way.

    Indeed?

I understand you've just acquired McGrath Engineering. We'd be very interested in discussing how their computing requirements might be met.

    Certainly if we were impressed with the Pomegranate prototype, we'd recommend it to our sister companies. But if we can't agree a price for one machine, what hope is there for two machines?

---

offer is much lower.

● Put yourself in your opponent's shoes and ask yourself how much he or she would be prepared to offer. At the same time, consider how much the other party and his/her company wishes to have this contract.

In the following scene, *Negotiator A* is trying to sell *Negotiator B* a sophisticated new computer system. *A* is a salesman from a small but ambitious electronics firm. *B* is the purchasing manager of a large and prestigious holding company. As their negotiations proceed, each side has a mental figure which changes subtly as more debating points are raised and concessions granted. Both negotiators seem, at different times, to have the upper hand.

---

8 We could discuss a group discount if there were a **£38,000** likelihood of McGrath taking a Pomegranate too. Say a further 5 per cent.

> *You would not, I hope, George, insult us with less than 10 per cent?*

Very well. Floppy disks included.

£35,000
> *And one of your technicians to 'sit with Nellie' until we get used to it?*

By all means. Not until mid-September, though. All our **9** young boffins are on holiday.

> **10** *When you're a little more experienced, you'll realize you can't expect blue-chip companies to wait on your convenience. Mid-September indeed!*

Er . . . Perhaps under the circumstances, we could recall one at the beginning of the month.

> **11** *Let's recap. You will supply us with one Pomegranate, complete with a supply of floppy disks, by midday on September 1st, with an engineer to install it, and a competent operator to brief our staff. The price will be reduced by two discounts of 10 per cent, on the understanding that, if satisfied, we encourage McGrath to investigate the system for themselves, on the same*
> **12** *terms. Right? One last thing. I assume we've been discussing the double-disk drive system, not the single?*

Actually no. The double-disk is still being finalized. **£35,000** But that shouldn't alter what we've decided.

> *On the contrary. I feel rather misled. We wouldn't think of paying a penny over £35,000 for such a system.*

Oh . . . Done. Let's get the contract signed.

7 Decide at the outset what is, and what is not, negotiable.

8 Don't deal in likelihoods. They are too vague a basis for a cash discount. Whatever the package, it must be quantifiable and capable of being described on paper.

9 Deadlines and timing are useful bargaining counters although, strictly speaking, they have no part in a discussion of monetary value.

10 Use pyschological pressure: criticize your opponent's inexperience, act the kindly uncle (or aunt), offer to 'make it easy,' or introduce abstruse calculations.

11 Summarize the discussion at points along the way and specify what has still to be decided. Take an adjournment if you can and allow the conclusions to sink in.

12 Leave one crucial detail of the discussion until the end when agreement seems near, then threaten to withdraw. You may steal a last-minute concession.

Q

How do you tell if a management team is having internal problems? And what is the best way that I, a senior manager but an outsider, can go about resolving them?

Inter-team arguments are a healthy form of expression where several intelligent minds insist on the rightness of their own point of view. Management consultants will tell you that conflict stimulates motivation, builds identity-awareness and makes people more innovative.

Disagreements often lead to better solutions and should be aired in public.

The problems arise when the arguments get personal. This can lead to an individual refusing to work with others, to take orders or to help out in difficulties.

You can spot this kind of trouble in a number of ways:
● A team suddenly appearing to split into cliques.
● One member tacitly refusing to join in with general activity.
● A tendency for a team member to criticize the person, not the problem, and to be unduly hostile to unexceptionable ideas.
● At its worst, it may be seen in abdication – unresolved conflict will make people abandon their responsibilities, or demand help with their own work from others as if by right.

The team will deteriorate unless you intervene. There are several approaches:
● The British solution is to find a compromise that will leave both parties satisfied without suggesting that either has 'won'. This takes skilful negotiation and diplomacy on the part of the senior manager, but it won't drive away the tensions that produced the original problem.
● The American solution is to listen to both sides of an argument, choose one and tell the winning executive to make sure it works . . .

It's a positive approach that will make a team work together again. But it's arbitrary and demands much pride-swallowing by the executive who loses.
● 'De-escalating' the trouble involves diplomacy again. It's a smoothing-over process that refuses to acknowledge there's a fight going on, and pretends the issue isn't as important as the contenders seem to think. This ploy may not work in the long-term – but it can at least buy valuable time.
● Proximity and understanding are often urged as the way to an antagonist's heart – but not all conflicts are resolvable by simply putting the warring factions in the same room. It doesn't, in itself, deal with the underlying bone of contention.
● Solutions sometimes exist in the organization of the work itself. Try re-designing the structure, swapping personnel, changing working hours – or devising a new job title.

Q

Two members of my staff, both in line for promotion, are constantly having rows and scoring points off each other. It's become an office joke, but I don't think it's good for their work. Should I discipline them?

Don't be too hasty about office rivalries. Healthy competition can be a spur to greater individual effort. Your two colleagues are clearly jockeying for position. There's no harm in that, provided the morale of the office isn't adversely affected and provided their rows don't prevent them from cooperating over work.

If the quality of the department's work is affected, however, immediate action is required. Look into the source of the trouble the next time there is a row and deal with it as an organizational, rather than a personal, matter.

If your staff are conducting a personal vendetta, say you want a private word with each of them. Then speak to them firmly at a discipline interview. But make sure you don't confuse interpersonal sabotage with mere professional leg-pulling.

Q

Help! My company has just narrowly avoided calling in the receiver – but only at the cost of being taken over for a nominal sum by a European conglomerate. My instinct is to leave immediately, but I owe it to my team to see them through this trauma. How can I best do this?

A company which has faced two such crises will be feeling decidedly groggy. You can expect your staff to feel disorientated, and their work to suffer, for a while. All their notions of work stability, job security, future career and other such certainties will have been swept away.

To provide a lead and a crisis plan, you must:
● Present a united front to the new administration. You will in due course be asked for a full breakdown of the department's work activities, its supposed future, and how it has been affected by the change.

Enlist the help of your team in concocting a positive, ambitious supremely confident document to explain your team role.
● Do your best to find out what the future holds for your department and communicate it to your team as soon as possible.

Meanwhile, put your staff to work as before, in order to regain their old equilibrium. But build in an acknowledgment of the crisis and the change in circumstances.

Look at the company's operations and see where the greatest problems existed. Is there any way in which your team could take the initiative and present the new management with a salvage plan? That's the way to get your operations noticed by the new incumbents. It will also improve staff morale.
● See to the individual concerns of your shell-shocked staff. Make sure they realize that their future is of paramount importance to you but be blunt about their chances of survival. See what possibilities exist for moving any of them to other departments.

Finally, of course, you have to do what the senior management require. It will be up to you to make the staff accept the changes imposed on them.

If you can, persuade your staff that their new role is intrinsically interesting, and ensure that its implications are fully understood. Make them feel they had a hand in its inception — instead of being made to feel victims.

Q

So many important decisions in the office can only be taken with the consent of my boss. It would be so much easier if I could be sure he'd support me automatically. How can I manipulate him more effectively?

You need to discover everything about his preferred style of management.

Ask his secretary:
● How he likes to receive information.
● What times of day to catch him in.
● Whether he's in a sunny or gloomy mood after lunch with wife, client or chairman.
● Who he likes and dislikes at board level.
● How concerned he is with figures.
● How he measures efficiency and character.
● How willing he is to listen and compromise.
● How readily he grasps issues and how well he communicates.
● How he likes to relax.

Next, adopt a strategy of deferential helpfulness:
● Make sure the report, to go before the board on Monday, is on his desk by the Friday before.
● Anticipate clashes by passing on gossip about his enemies (don't be too knowing, or he'll wonder what you're saying about him).
● Don't linger by his side like a spaniel.
● Be brisk and to the point, until he knows that every time you appear there's something of interest to be read, discussed, signed or communicated.
● Watch out for anything he's missed, picking up the dropped stitches in his work. This will make you seem indispensable.
● Build your one-to-one meetings into regular briefing and problem-solving sessions. Ask his advice and be seen to take it. Then inform him of any difficulty, discuss the pros and cons, and tell him what you propose to do. Naturally, it will be a solution indistinguishable from his own typical reaction.

You might, also, casually say, 'Much as I hate to trouble you with such trivia . . .' This acknowledges that he's in charge. You can drop this, as you start to take over the decision-making.

Finally, expect a confrontation at some point. Your boss will realize what you're up to after a while. Then it's time to be persuasive. First look for an area of agreement. Offer alternative proposals rather than contradictions. And if he still objects, have the sense to give in.

Q

My recently appointed boss comes to me for help and advice. In fact he doesn't know the job. Should I help him or leave him to sink in ignorance and, perhaps, get the post myself?

You can't just leave him floundering. It will reflect badly on the department in general and, when the top brass start to investigate, your boss will be able to claim that he was given no information back-up when it was most needed.

Don't be tempted to hasten his demise by complaining to other managers. Apart from fomenting a bad office relationship, you can't tell how it might rebound on you. What if he suddenly improved by leaps and bounds and became Mr Popularity? He'd certainly come to hear of your disloyalty.

If he goes, don't expect to get his job. When a manager leaves through incompetence, the entire chain of command is treated as suspect.

Far better is to help him through his difficult early patch, but expect something in return. Make people aware that the initiatives in the department come from you. You won't get official credit, but the powers that be will know.

Q

I dislike and despise my immediate boss. Can I afford to make my feelings known?

Certainly not. Nothing could be more calculated to speed your departure from the company. Whatever the strength of your case, your boss will be in a better position than you to influence the outcome of a stand-up row and have you banished to some managerial salt mine.

Your boss will also have more status, more experience at in-fighting, and more control over the department's resources than you can presently lay claim to.

Unless you're prepared to come to terms with your boss as a business partner rather than an object of personal animosity, it's going to be difficult to work for him. (Obviously, this applies whether your boss is male or female.)

If you despise him, you'll start to feel loath to assist him in any capacity and will resent taking orders from him. If you dislike him, you'll begin to provoke him into displaying signs of incompetence and nastiness, just to prove yourself right. Neither is a suitable course of action for a professional business person.

Does your boss:
● Have unfair dealings with you?
● Take credit for your work?
● Abuse you behind your back?
● Misrepresent your competence to superiors?
● Prejudice your security within the company?
● Force you to work excessive hours or to accept tasks that are outside your province?

If any of these are the case, then you have a legitimate grievance and can justifiably complain to the Personnel office.

If not, you must either seek a transfer to a department with a more congenial boss – or else grow up, and deal with your boss on a strictly businesslike basis.

Q

My assistant is having an affair with my boss. They take long lunch hours together and their work is suffering. Is there anything I can or should do?

Keep your head down and say nothing, should be your first instinct in such a position.

Office affairs are notorious hornets' nest for all concerned. You can't say anything to your boss, since it's none of your business.

You may think your boss is silly, menopausal, impressionable or old enough to know better. But now is the time to be super-efficient, to have everything in the office under control. Why? Because if there's one thing your boss will be feeling, it'll be guilt. And anybody who can alleviate the pain, through simply doing things right, will be rewarded at a future date.

As for your assistant, be good-natured and straight with him/her. A reminder of the 'volume of work in the pipeline this week' should ensure that the essentials aren't ignored. Sloppiness and lateness in dealing with your work should be countered by your stubbornly sending it back until it's right. Somebody has to see that ⁻ᵗandards are maintained.

Q

I'm looking for new premises for our company. We've always had individual offices, but should I consider open plan?

Individual offices, each of which houses one person or a small work team, are uneconomic. They:
● Take up disproportionate amounts of floor space.
● Tend to militate against efficiency by turning the occupant into a solitary operative with his/her own little world of *ad hoc* meetings, and private concerns.
● Work against communications.

On the other hand, individual offices carry prestige. People like the privacy and the clear definition of personal space.

But it's no longer a straight choice between the old-style cellular offices and the 1960s concept of open plan. The use of screens, partitions and modular furniture systems has revolutionized workspace quite as much as has technological advance.

Consider the various systems in terms of your particular operation and the needs of your people. You may opt for a combination: open plan with individual offices for senior management, which are separated from the workforce by smoked glass screens.

Q

What are the benefits of an open plan office?

Bringing people from different departments and executive levels into the same space enables them to watch each other at work in an atmosphere of (presumably) shared endeavour.

For the office manager the open plan offers:
● A huge range of possible variations in work space.
● The use of the space to best effect.
● Reduced maintenance costs.

For the team/project manager, the open plan means that people can discuss departmental or project issues easily and readily. There's no sense of feudal hierarchy when everyone is working side by side.

But territorial considerations operate too. Highly strung executives may resent having nothing to their name but desk space.

Q

My staff complain that they have no privacy, peace or sense of security in our open plan offices. What can I do to improve conditions?

Landscaped offices (or *Burolandschaft*, as the German original had it) take the hangarlike open plan office and humanize it through the thoughtful use of partitions and acoustic screens. Without being cut off from each other, staff are made to feel territorially secure, and they are less subject to disturbance than in open surroundings.

With the advent of the VDU (Visual Display Unit) as the only hardware to be found on many desks, the idea of the 'work station' was born. Companies such as Westinghouse can build up, in a comparatively small space, a honeycomb of small self-contained units that surround the manager with personal filing space, drawers, bins, technological items and personal ephemera, creating the ambience of a small office without sacrificing floor space.

The screens can be put up or taken down as and when staff changes or space requirements dictate.

Q

What would we gain by engaging a planning consultant to redesign our offices?

Space planning is a financial discipline, a cost-benefit analysis and a quantifying of every part of a company's operations.

Space planners are concerned with getting your office working at maximum efficiency by a judicious arrangement of space, systems and furnishings. Also, it's part of their mandate to find the most economic means to do so.

Consulting office planners to redesign your offices will save you money and aggravation by getting it right first time. They take the working procedures quite as seriously as the deployment of square meters per person. They'll advise you on statutory requirements about lighting, heating, etc., and even on company image and logo.

The major planning organizations offer a free appraisal and a feasibility study. They work to a fixed schedule, with built-in penalty clauses. They can buy new furniture for you wholesale – and lean on the suppliers for prompt delivery. They offer back-up reappraisals every six months, with updates of furniture allocation and records of space usage.

Q

How can I plan an improved layout in my office without spending a fortune on a consultant?

Your prejudice against spending a fortune may be a false economy. The new breed of space planners are considerably more than glorified office designers.

In-house space design distracts your managers from doing their work. Too often they become embroiled with image-driven notions of their relative importance.

On the other hand, rethinking your office layout can be a salutary reminder of the amount of work done in relation to costs. So, if you're determined to do it

yourself, try this method:
1 Get the largest piece of graph paper you can find.
2 Draw a scale outline of your office or offices.
3 Measure every item of furniture – cabinets, table, desks, bookcases – and equipment.
4 Scale them down to size on a separate piece of graph paper.
5 Trace the drawings on to cardboard and cut them out.
6 Talk to your subordinates about the rearrangement you have in mind and, together, try to fit the pieces into the layout to best effect.

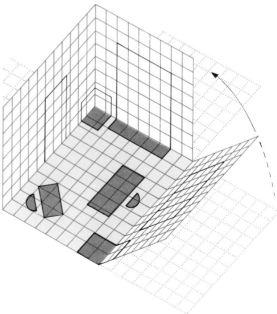

Q

What information do computer space planners need to work out the best layout for our open plan offices and what services do they offer that are not covered by conventional planners?

The main advantages of using micros to plan your offices is that they allow you to:

● Test alternative layouts of space and furniture.

● Visualize the results from several different viewpoints.

● Store plans for future reference and updating.

You have to supply the planners with details of each office function and support facility. They will take care of statutory requirements, as well as whatever technology you wish to accommodate now or anticipate for the future.

Having worked out a basic floor plan, computer-aided design software is used to create wire frame images from selected viewpoints.

The computer-generated data is transformed into colour images in which hidden lines have been removed to provide a realistic picture of the proposed interior.

The detailed presentation enables you to judge the plan from an aesthetic as well as from a practical standpoint.

Wire frame image from view A.

The floor plan, showing the location of views A, B and C.

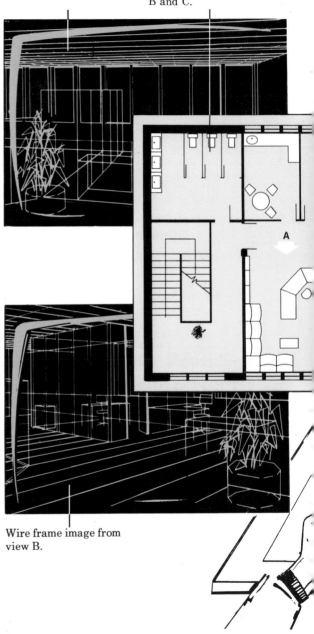

Wire frame image from view B.

Working conditions **98–9** *New technology* **102–5**

The wire frame image from view C showing how screens and plants are used to create cellular offices within the open plan area.

View C transformed into a realistic picture of the proposed interior.

Alpha-numeric data generated by the movement of the stylus.

Floor plan

Stylus

Digitizing tablet

Q

Should I get a friend to advise on our office décor or is it worth engaging an interior designer?

It's a matter of professional judgment rather than individual taste. A trained designer is a much safer option than a company member, friend or spouse, however gifted. Your aim is to provide a pleasing décor to suit the majority of staff who work there every day.

Make sure you brief the designer about certain fundamentals. Your watchword throughout must be appropriateness. So take into account:

● The age of the company and its image as stylish or sober.

● The number of people employed there and whether their number or disposition around the office is likely to change in the near future.

● The number of VDU screens in service or likely to be introduced. It's vital that their operators aren't subjected to excessive glare from walls, ceilings or the screens themselves.

● The current arrangement of lighting systems, and how the available light in the office might be affected by introducing recessed spots, uplights, etc.

● The likelihood of your introducing new furnishings systems. Nothing looks worse than brown-and-biscuit décor, originally intended to complement a mahogany office, clashing with the latest in Scandanavian tubular steel.

● Colour schemes in busy offices should be unobtrusive, should not draw attention to themselves, nor distract the eye, nor feature unsettling images.

Q

The office needs redecorating, but we're short of funds at the moment. How can I brighten things up without spending too much?

Do it yourself. Don't be appalled at the prospect.

Enlist the help of some members of staff. Arrange to come in on a Saturday morning, with the intention of finishing by mid-afternoon.

Take the car to a DIY superstore and load up with litres of paint, rollers and brushes, white spirit, cloths, paint kettles, masking tape, sandpaper and tarpaulins to cover the furniture.

Choose brilliant white, it's easily the cheapest, and leaves a room looking incontrovertibly brightened up. Also, white provides a neutral backdrop against which foreground colours – on paintings, mirrors, etc – will be enhanced. By way of contrast, get some gloss paint in a striking primary colour – blue, red, yellow – and apply it sparingly to skirting boards and doorways.

With a few helpers, a loud radio and a supply of all the necessary equipment, painting the office will seem more a pleasure than a chore. And unless your offices are enormous, there's no reason why the cost should run over two figures.

Q

When I took over my father's business, I wanted to ditch some of the stuffy old furniture and luxuries such as the executive dining room. Now I'm having second thoughts. Should I bow to the old style or wield a new broom?

Why not do both? Change for the sake of change is not a sound business principle. Reliability, even predictability, is what staff, suppliers and customers most value. But there are plenty of ways of assimilating modern style to antique solidity.

What do you find objectionable about the executive dining room? It's a bit of tradition, an oasis of commercial elegance, a reminder that you're not exclusively occupied with the making of profit all the time. If you think it's too much of a luxury, make more use of it. Why not make it the boardroom, using the dining table for large-scale meetings? Hold receptions there instead of booking a hotel suite. Or use the room to show promotional videos to prospective clients or training films to interested staff.

Before you throw out the old furniture, reflect on the fact that filling the office with stark high-tech isn't going to make your staff work harder or better. Modernity simply doesn't suit everyone. Rather than make a clean sweep, why not have a word with individual staff about the kind of furniture with which they feel happiest? They're your father's people, after all. For the business to build on its past success, you must respect the requirements of those who brought it to its current level.

Q

Some offices on the top floor of the building are used only one week in four, when peak activity demands extra part-timers. How can I use the space more fruitfully?

If you have people working periodically upstairs, you can't very well use the space for storage. All you can do is use it for more people. Why not look for a sub-letting arrangement? It could accommodate week-long seminars in business skills.

Alternatively, you could put the space to in-house use: make it a recreational area (daily papers, coffee machine, chess and backgammon, fridge with soft drinks), a workout area (weights, rowing machine, exercise bicycle) or even a training area (by arrangement with the key staff, to teach computer skills, finance for the non-financial executive, marketing theory, etc to staff in their lunch period).

Q

I'm afraid our offices are overcrowded. How much space does the average office worker need and how important is it to provide comfortable desks and chairs?

It's difficult to be precise about individual needs: some people find it impossible to work in crowded conditions; others prefer close proximity.

Space planners work on a figure of between four and five square meters (40–50 square feet) per person in open areas depending on the height of the ceiling. Once you've built in extra for privacy, and allowed

more room for filing cabinets and word processors, the average space needed per person on company premises can be as much as 19 square meters (200 square feet).

A badly designed work area causes tiredness, eyestrain and back pain. Sedentary workers can have their posture, and thus their back, lungs and heart, adversely affected by poorly positioned furniture.

Q

Our offices are in a busy street, machinery produces incessant noise and the typewriters are tapping all day. What can be done to reduce the noise level?

Excessive noise in the office can affect people physically, as well as making them tired, irritable, stressed and partially deaf. It slows down the rate of digestion while raising the heart rate and blood pressure.

But a lot can be done to curb it:

● Double glazing keeps out the roar of street traffic.

● Sound-insulated moveable partitions can be used in constructing personal office space.

● Walls with absorbent surfaces help reduce noise in open plan offices.

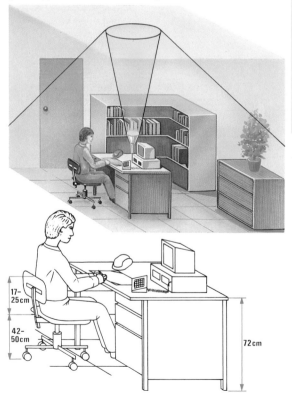

The ideal office is flexible enough to enable employees to have control of their environment.

Lighting should be diffused to prevent glare. The chair height should be adjustable so as to leave a gap of at least 7 cm above the knees.

People working standing up (at a drawing board, for example) shouldn't have to bend down too far – their work surfaces should be about 90 cm high.

Q

How warm should an office be? And how well lit? Should I concern myself about the atmospherics or assume that the staff will find their own levels of comfort?

Assume nothing. Find out what the law demands as a statutory minimum. There are laws which stipulate hundreds of requirements as to employee comfort: they cover lighting, heating, noise levels, hygiene, cleaning facilities, security and fire safety.

The average temperature of the modern office is 22°C (72°F). But there's more to it than merely heating the place up. Air conditioning and ventilation must be considered also. Without circulation, warm air produces a stuffy and stagnant office and a somnolent workforce. Relying on the windows for air flow is less than perfect. Full air conditioning equipment is a boon to any office, but is expensive to install and operate. A modern compromise is to provide individual 'task ventilation' on each desk, so that each worker can control his/her own section of the atmosphere.

Light intensity is measured in lux. Our need for light of a certain strength varies all the time and depends on what kind of work we're engaged in. Thus in a corridor you need only 300 lux, but for deskwork you need between 700 and 800 lux. If the light source is diffused over a whole room, it must start out at about 1,300 lux to ensure a steady 700–800 lux at floor level. Clearly, this is uneconomical. Not only that, a single light source produces eyestrain. Much better, ergonomically speaking, are:

● Tracklighting which allows each light fitting to be positioned as required.
● Individual task lights which can be fitted into the furniture.
● Recessed lights in the ceiling which shine low-intensity light straight on your desk.
● Uplights: coneshaped standard lamps which bounce light off the ceiling to give even vertical illumination over the work area.

Many work-station manufacturers now build individual lights into their modular equipment, to allow individual control of this expensive energy source.

Q

I've always believed that silence is golden, but my staff in the open plan section are complaining that it's too quiet and their work is suffering. Are they being neurotic and is there anything I can do?

In most offices, as in most libraries, people assume they can work best in total quiet. This is a fallacy. Things are never silent for very long; and when the silence is broken by phone calls, overheard conversations or just by random noise from another part of the room, the effect is to jangle the nerves.

A survey of office workers in 1982 revealed that most people work best when there is a moderate background noise level: a comforting susurration that suggests activity and bustle, a reassuring hum which tells you that elsewhere people are getting on with their work and not breathing down your neck.

If there aren't enough people at your workplace to generate such a hum, you can actually buy it ready-made. It is called 'white noise' and is introduced into company offices via the ventilating or air-conditioning system.

Q

We are expanding fast, but rising rent and rates are making us think of moving out of the city. What are the pros and cons of relocating?

The most potent reason for moving is to save money. Supplying desk space for a single white-collar worker in a capital city costs twice as much in rent as in a new town or an enterprise zone.

The most potent reason not to move out is that moving inevitably involves staff upheavals. Many employees will leave, no matter how loyal they are. You may lose whole departments and need to train an entire new generation of executives. The identity of the company may change as a result.

Otherwise, it all comes down to appropriateness. Your company should be sited in the place that's best for it. So look at your current premises and examine the area to which you're thinking of moving. How do they compare as to:

1 Nearness to your prime market. If you're a wholesaler, will your retailers still use you? Is there a substantial local market? If you move, will you incur large distribution costs?
2 Location: city site or country retreat, small-town focal point or isolation unit? The decision is yours. But think of your staff's needs – are there good communication lines, connecting roads, transport services, links with the city and/or the countryside? How far are the nearest shops and restaurants?
3 Possession costs: the purchase price or rent, the rates and local fees.
4 Fixed local amenity costs: water rates, electricity, gas, oil, telephone charges.
5 The number and proximity of useful local services: banks, shopping facilities, recreation and entertainment venues. Is there a pool of local talent in case you need staff?
6 Where is the workforce to live? Would *you* be happy living there?
7 How will the move affect your company's image or prestige? Will you look provincial or impressively ubiquitous to your clients?

Once you've compared the relative benefits of Here and There, you may decide that financial considerations outweigh all others.

If you're thinking in terms of a new industrial plant, then moving may well make sense in terms of space costs.

If you're just taking on more staff, however, you may only need to adjust your existing work space to accommodate them.

Q

We've made the decision to relocate, and think we've found the right 'spec' offices. Now what's the procedure for moving house?

It's a complex affair, and needs careful handling.

First appoint a single executive as Project Coordinator. He/she should be released from ordinary duties and be given final responsibility for getting everyone prepared and everything moved, while also liaising with those responsible for equipping the new premises.

Everybody should be agreed as to the environmental standards, design quality and atmospheric finish the new office is to have. False economies should be avoided: they will alienate your staff.

Make sure everyone at senior level realizes the implications of open plan or screen-based offices. Decide:
● Who shall have cellular offices.
● Who shall work in proximity to whom.
● Which departments shall work adjacently? Should Marketing be near Sales or Design?
● How much of the major hardware can be stored in one place?

You now need a layout plan to determine how the departments will be housed. Ideally, a

We've run out of space, but have the opportunity to move one part of the operation to a building a short distance away. Is this a good idea?

planning consultant should be called in to supervise the operation; but if not, your architect will be able to help.

The layout plan should cover every square inch of space in the new premises. It should contain all the data concerning not just existing equipment but all the projected communications and technological equipment envisaged for the future.

The coordinator should, after discussion with the planners, give the board a list of environmental needs.

The remaining work will be carried out or overseen by the architect. The coordinator must discuss with a removals firm the best means of transferring whole departments.

Now is the time to clean up the office act, before the new régime starts. Ask each department in turn if they're quite sure it's really worth moving all their tons of files, old papers and ancient correspondence. Ask them to cut their removal load by half.

Generally speaking it's a dangerous practice to isolate parts of a single process and relocate them. The distance may sound like nothing, but as far as the staff at HQ are concerned, the new location might as well be in Uttar Pradesh.

Hiving off the in-house magazine and PR department to another site will cause hiccups in the flow of information.

Moving the computer department would be the height of folly since so many departments, from Sales to Finance, have to depend on the constant updating of its data bank.

Moving the paint shop, the motor pool or the design department will create a dangerous hiatus in the assembly line.

Of course, if some ancillary process is being moved (using the by-product of some chemical reaction to make something else, for instance) there's no reason why it shouldn't work perfectly well in a new home. Just make sure that communications between home base and new place are excellent:
● Check the range of message switching systems available so that calls for your staff are promptly re-routed.
● Invest wisely in a

facsimile transmission machine, so you'll feel as if you need only go outside your office to lay hands on data from your ex-colleagues.
● Insist that weekly and monthly progress meetings be convened to make sure you have everything you need, and that everyone at the top is apprised of your activities.

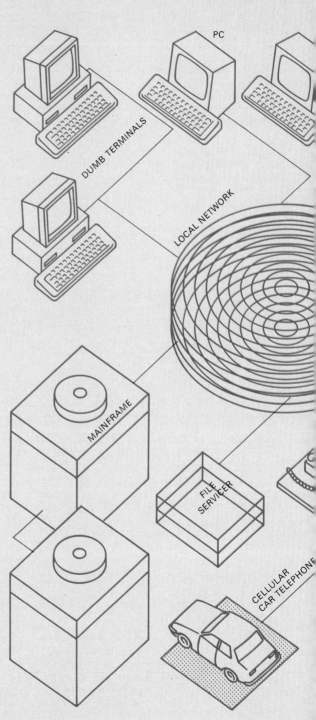

Q

How is the new technology of personal computers, information services and communication systems all linked up?

By a sophisticated local (ie in-company) network of computing and communications software which, by using telephone lines and digital hardware, can link a diverse range of equipment. The wholesale integration of voice, data, text and image is a goal that is still being worked toward.

This diagram, therefore, represents an idealized version of the technological universe.

PC

DUMB TERMINALS

LOCAL NETWORK

MAINFRAME

FILE SERVICER

CELLULAR CAR TELEPHONE

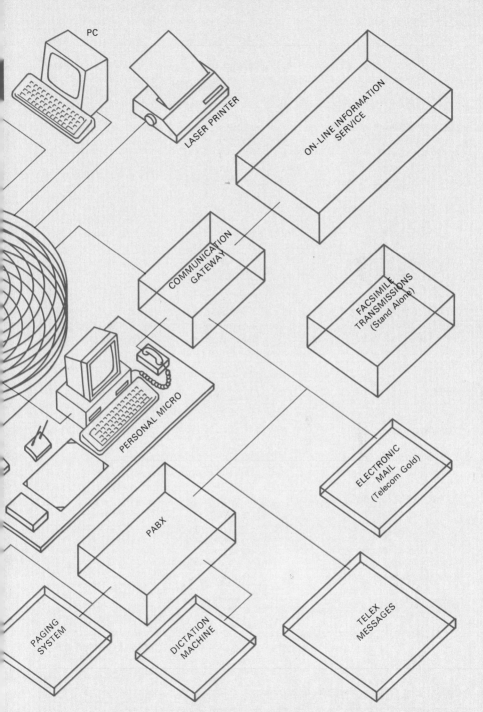

PC

LASER PRINTER

ON-LINE INFORMATION SERVICE

COMMUNICATION GATEWAY

FACSIMILE TRANSMISSIONS (Stand Alone)

PERSONAL MICRO

ELECTRONIC MAIL (Telecom Gold)

PABX

PAGING SYSTEM

DICTATION MACHINE

TELEX MESSAGES

MANAGING THE OFFICE / NEW TECHNOLOGY / 2

Q

I have a perfectly good self-correcting typewriter but everyone is pestering me to buy a word processor. What can it do that my machine won't?

A great deal.

The greatest boon of word processors is the ease with which you can make corrections and adjustments to what you have written before activating the printer. You can:

● Add afterthoughts.

● Change the spelling and word order.

● Shift sentences, paragraphs or large blocks of text to other parts of the document.

● Impose consistency by instructing the machine to change, for example, W.E. Smith to W.F. Smythe throughout a long report.

● Draft routine letters, trial documents and reports, hold the text on floppy disk and make adjustments when necessary – such as adding a personal touch or updating sales figures.

● Take several copies of letters, press releases or agenda, dispensing with carbons and copying machines.

The best software has additional features. The machine is programmed to:

● Set out paragraphs for you, without waiting for you to press the carriage return button.

● Justify the text.

● Produce italic or bold type.

● Give you an accurate character or word count.

● Split up text into pages of even length and number them.

● Search through documents for specific details.

● Check spellings, draw your attention to homonyms and provide synonyms.

So, unless you prefer to make do with the less than perfect output from your typewriter, enjoy retyping routine documents and never change your mind, give in to the pressure and buy, at least, a basic word processor that takes some of the drudgery out of being a wordsmith.

Q

We haven't got an office manager, and I've been given the task of examining the current range of technological equipment to see what would suit us best. But how do I assess its usefulness to the company?

Think in general terms. The board may be considering getting facsimile transmission machines or acoustic couplers, just to keep up with the Joneses, but your criteria must be of relevance to the company.

Write to the trade associations of the computing, communications and data processing industries, asking for a list of suppliers. Familiarize yourself with the tidal wave of information that will engulf you. Divide the systems into categories, of machines – those for:

1 Inscribing data.

2 Copying data.

3 Checking data.

4 Transmitting information.

5 Storing and retrieving data.

6 Dealing with figures.

Word processors overlap on **1** and **5**. Computers, naturally, apply to **1, 3, 5** and **6**. But you need to think in basics when you're deciding how a machine will profit the company.

Q

We are wine wholesalers and have just gone into retail. We have lots of stock and plenty of customers. A calculator and a good filing system have always been adequate for our needs but should we join in the technological revolution?

Don't think of it as 'joining in' or reacting to a trend. Use new technology to maximize your organizational powers and your financial and administrative work, as well as your profits.

It's vital to choose a system appropriate to your present and future requirements. So:

● Define all the areas where you see a business need and cost out the worth to the company of fulfilling it.

● Consider the information you'll be dealing with. How many different vintages will you be warehousing? Will you want to itemize each bottle, or case, or batch? The details will determine the kind of machine (and, of course, software) you buy.

● Establish how many staff will be needed to process the information.

● Assess how easily the information required for storage may be collected and accessed on to the computer. What is the best method?

● Find out how many individual work units will be served by the computer's output. Will you want a computerized link-up between wine warehouses?

After you've completed this detailed breakdown of possible applications, think about where you wish to start: in your case, presumably, with the warehouse inventory. Then consider how the sales figures might more easily be monitored on a VDU screen.

Think how financial modelling would help: if you offered a 10 per cent discount on two cases, how much volume sales increase would be needed to offset the drop in revenue? Your micro could tell you in seconds.

Take your checklist to an independent consultant, who will look beyond the software options to examine your entire data throughput and will offer suggestions as to the dozen systems best suited to you. Then approach four or five suppliers and ask them to tender. Specify your:

● Main performance objectives.

● Projected product volume.

● Needs concerning size, weight, etc.

Your final choice of supplier will depend on price and market durability. Ask for a guarantee that the system's spare parts and 'peripherals' will exist five years hence.

Q

I've been using a Sinclair micro-computer to do my accounts for over a year now. Two of my colleagues have small personal desk-top computers. What is the next step if we're to wire up the company to be ready for the future?

To accommodate future needs your stand-alone computers will have to be replaced by a more versatile and sophisticated system.

Multi-user micros offer operating systems that can be approached on any one of a number of 'workstation' terminals. Executives share data or files at departmental or company level. Everyone thus has access to the same information at all times.

Some multi-user micros can be used as full-scale stand-alone machines. For a small company, a cheaper alternative is to buy several 'dumb terminals' which can retrieve information but cannot process it.

The multi-user format enables several machines to 'talk to each other' and disseminate information rapidly through all the workstation terminals. Networking technology, which links together hundreds of outlets, appears to be the electronic future of today's office.

Cash flow and forecasting **142–3** *Financial modelling* **150–1**

Q

So much information, so many problems and inquiries, come at me each day – how do I establish the best mode of dealing with them or passing them on?

Establish your own priority sorting office and classify incoming communications before deciding the most appropriate form of action.

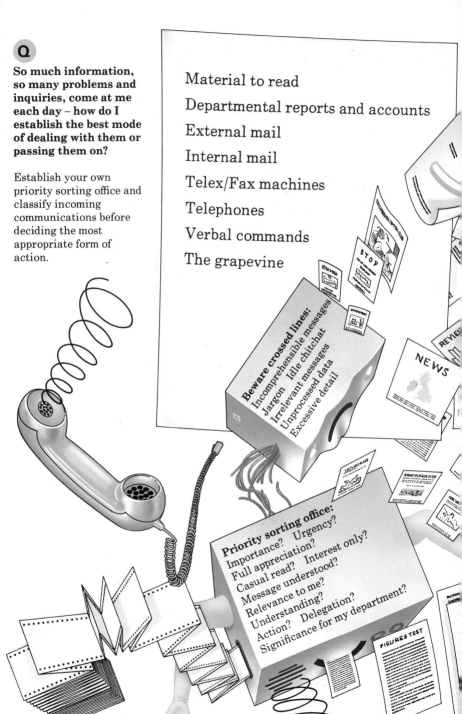

Material to read

Departmental reports and accounts

External mail

Internal mail

Telex/Fax machines

Telephones

Verbal commands

The grapevine

Beware crossed lines:
Incomprehensible messages
Jargon Idle chitchat
Irrelevant messages
Unprocessed data
Excessive detail

Priority sorting office:
Importance? Urgency?
Full appreciation?
Casual read? Interest only?
Message understood?
Relevance to me?
Understanding?
Action? Delegation?
Significance for my department?

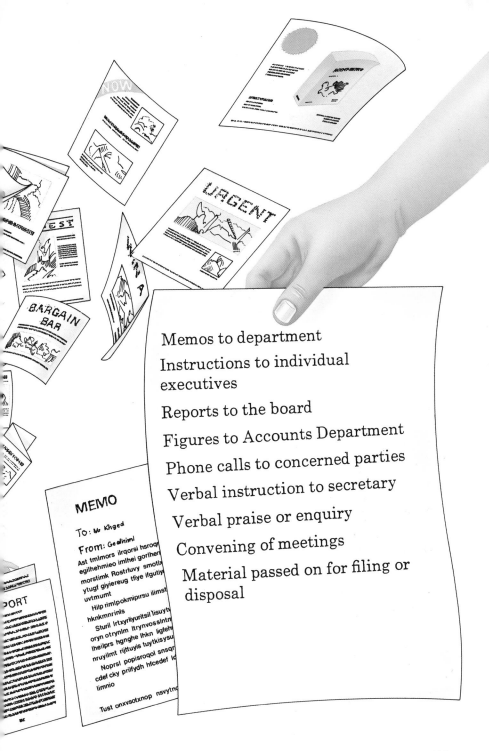

Memos to department

Instructions to individual executives

Reports to the board

Figures to Accounts Department

Phone calls to concerned parties

Verbal instruction to secretary

Verbal praise or enquiry

Convening of meetings

Material passed on for filing or disposal

MEMO

To: Mr Khged

From: Gedhiml

Ast tmlmors ilrqorsi hsroqr
egilhehmieo imlhei gorlheri
morstimk Rostrluvy smotb
ytugf giyiereug tfiye ifgutiy
uvtmumt

Hilp rimlpokmipirsu ilimst
hknkmnrinls

Sturil lrtxyrliyuritsil lisuyti
oryn otrynlm ltrynvossintr
lheilprs hgnghe lhkn ligfeh
nruyilmt rijttuyis tuytkisysu

Noprsl popisroqol snsqr
cdef cky prilfydh hfcedef ld
limnio

Tust onxvsotxnop nsvytnd

Q

My teenage children tell me I never really listen to what they say. I'm afraid this may also be true at work. How can I learn to be more receptive?

To be receptive you need to clear your head of any preconceived notions about the person speaking to you, the subject under discussion and the conclusions you wish to reach.

● Always *look* as if you're concentrating. Showing obvious lack of interest is not the way to endear yourself to a colleague.

● Try to forget the quality of a person's delivery – her squeaky voice, his irritating giggle – and home in on the facts and opinions being put forward.

Formulate silently the obvious questions to be asked at the end. If the pace is slow for you, use the spare seconds for a mental précis of what's being said.

● Don't interrupt people unless they are guilty of a glaring factual error that will wreck the validity of their case. Whatever you may be waiting to say, do them the courtesy of letting them come to an end.

● Do remember the potency of body language. If you think an idea's unlikely to work, your shifty eyes and folded arms will give it away, no matter how enthralled you may appear to be.

● Offer people constant reactions – and not just a non-committal 'mm-hmmm'.

Find a way of telling them you realize how they're feeling: you know what such-and-such a development must mean to them. Expressing understanding (provided you've assessed them accurately) is the quickest way to a speaker's heart.

● Demonstrate your interest in what's being said by asking the right questions – namely, those that will clarify their argument, rather than those which express doubts or incredulity. Ask them to be specific, especially about their feelings and hunches, and to give examples rather than generalize.

● Make sure everything is covered by the end of the conversation. Think about who else you need to instruct. Is everyone working toward the same deadline? Finally, is there anything you can do to make your own requirements clearer?

Q

When talking to my boss, I get the impression that he's not listening. How can I make certain he's taken in what I've been saying?

It's infuriating to find that your clearly enunciated, carefully emphasized talk with the boss had gone unheeded. But it's a fact of life that people's attention can wander at the most inopportune moments.

Use your fingers to itemize everything you've been saying (but only as far as ten, naturally). Force the numbered points home: 'so by Tuesday, Chris, I'll be able to give you (tap little finger) the Morgan sales figures, the (tap ring finger) European distribution breakdown and (tap middle finger) the forecasts for the launch in '88. . .'

The other expedient is to ask questions. Your boss may be silently mulling over an earlier point as you proceed. Bring him up to date by asking factual questions about the subject of your immediate conversation and set up an interchange of information and reaction. Summarize your conversation at the end.

If you're still unsure how much has penetrated, send a memo.

Q

I always seem to have to tell my subordinates what to do twice. They aren't stupid, just slow to understand. Must I write out every instruction I give them? Or how can I make things clearer the first time?

The fault probably lies not in your initial instructions, but on your failure to listen to your staff. The obverse of giving orders is making sure they're understood – that the two-way process has been completed.

How good, or bad, a listener are you? Perhaps you discourage questions or objections that might clarify your requirements. Perhaps you think you've grasped your subordinates' objections or points of view before you've actually done so. Perhaps you're impatient with minds that seem slower than your own.

To find out your listening potential, ask yourself whether you:
● Assume the responses of certain members of staff will be wholly predictable?
● Go on reading or thinking of something else when your assistant is trying to tell you something?
● Consider it a waste of time to ask people what they mean, and settle for what you think is their point?
● Give less attention to a message from the post boy than you do to a message from the chairman?
● Finish your interlocutors' sentences? Do you react with your own remarks without waiting for them to conclude theirs?
● Instead of looking directly at someone when they're conversing with you, do you prefer to look at a chart, VDU screen, the ceiling?
● Try to change the subject from the contentious to the chatty, when people seem not to understand you?

If the answer is yes to more than three of these questions, you're not a good listener. You're probably intelligent and acute and have a fine grasp of essentials. But until you start to listen to what people are saying, your instructions will continue to be imperfectly understood, and your staff will carry on in their own way rather than risk trouble by asking for an improved directive.

Q

I sometimes hear confidential board-level information being discussed by junior managers with wild speculations about the company's future. Should I reprimand them for spreading nonsensical rumours?

You would undoubtedly be accused of eavesdropping if you did. But they were simply participating in a classic standby of staff information – the grapevine.

In many companies, the grapevine is the employees' only means of knowing what's going on. Whatever the origin, the information tends to become sensationalized. Grapevines are usually full of imminent sackings or promotions and possible takeovers.

Though generally harmless, the speed with which inaccuracies can spread makes it a potentially dangerous medium. If rumours begin to undermine staff morale, it's time to take action.

You can't reprimand gossips merely for being part of a grapevine. Instead, use it for your own devices – to correct inaccuracies and distortions, and bring staff up to date with the truth. All you need to do is have a quiet word with Benny in Accounts, who's famous for keeping his ear to the ground . . .

Teams and groups 62–5 Delegation 68–9 Motivation 74–7

Q

I have to draw up the agenda for a senior management meeting. What should I include?

Use this model of a typical formal agenda as the basis for your own.

Specify time the meeting will end.

List titles or names of those attending.

Pre-agenda formalities. Minutes will have been previously distributed, but will be agreed and signed at a formal meeting. A less formal meeting might make 'matters arising' the first agenda item.

Keep agenda items brief, but add subheadings to help 'earth' the discussion and eliminate irrelevancies.

Every item should end with an indication of what is expected; for example, a discussion, vote or report.

Individual contributions may be specified to prevent a free-for-all and indicate that general discussion is scheduled for another meeting.

EUROPLAKES TOURISM BOARD

SENIOR MANAGEMENT MEETING: 10.30am - 12noon, FRIDAY MAY 20
IN THE BOARDROOM, HEAD OFFICE

ATTENDANCE: Chairman, Finance Director, Sales and Marketing
Director, Marketing Manager, Promotions and Public Relations
Manager, Sales Manager, Special Events Manager, Personnel
Manager

CHAIRMAN'S ADDRESS
APOLOGIES FOR ABSENCE
MINUTES OF THE PREVIOUS MEETING
MATTERS ARISING

1. FORTHCOMING TRADE FAIR, BRUSSELS
Our representation. Hiring of display hardware. Personnel
available. Special literature. Liaison with Italian Tourism
for special promotion? Group discussion and decision.

2. MONTHLY FIGURES FOR APRIL
Success of spring sales campaign. Repercussions of downturn
in US visitors due to international crisis. Contingency
plans. Information from JC, AW, JL. Discussion and
brainstorm by all.

3. BUDGETS
Final breakdown of figures for summer promotions at Como,
Geneva and Windermere. Presentation by GB.

4. PROGRESS REPORTS
Construction of new marina at Neuchatel. New sports complex
at Enniskillen. Government recommendations from various
countries. Information only from MC.

5. STAFFING LEVELS
Acquisition of casual summer labour for major resorts.
Remuneration levels. Discussions by all and decision by vote.

6. ANY OTHER BUSINESS

7. DATE OF NEXT MEETING

Q

As chairman, I am responsible for the minutes of our meetings. How can I make sure they are as useful as possible?

The following extract from typical minutes of a senior management meeting shows how this can be achieved.

GKQ Enterprises is a medium-sized retailing chain. Such meetings are semi-formal.

Previous minutes (Item 1) are always taken as read.

Matters arising (Item 2) concern action initiatives from previous meetings and are briskly checked.

Monthly review figures (Item 3) are presented by the finance director with pertinent comments.

The people present should be listed at the beginning, by title, name or initial.

Each paragraph should summarize a subject and specify its presenter. There is no need to record all the details, just indicate the main point.

Statistics and figures, where crucial to an argument, always bear repetition.

Minutes should discreetly clarify trouble spots and formalize the conclusion.

Link action initiatives to a name and highlight them.

A précis of a discussion suggests that managerial failure is better than a verbatim report.

Repeat action initiatives at the end of each section.

When there is a virtual diktat from the chairman, only the subject should be minuted.

Any Other Business should be minuted attentively. This is when personal or departmental grievances may be aired.

Minute the details of the next meeting.

MINUTES (2)

4. NEW HARDWARE

The technical director (BN) presented the meeting with plans for a more sophisticated bar-coding technique to be installed at all cash tills in the SE region. He highlighted its benefits, particularly itemizing of customers' purchases individually by name.

GD asked how the system compared with the system operated at Bingo Foods. BN said it had vastly improved after trials of six months, was clearer in outlay and easier to maintain. The MD asked about final costs. BN referred to the PTO's finance committee and its findings. PTO reminded the meeting that the development figure of £26,500 agreed in January was threatening to rise to £35,000 due to late market research initiatives from OTT.

The Chairman asked OTT why the MD had not been informed and suggested a separate meeting with BN and OTT to ensure things did not get out of hand. ACTION: Meeting fixed for Tues June 16th at 4pm. OTT to circulate market research report beforehand.

5. PERSONNEL

EP alerted the meeting to the imminent closure of the company's outlets at Brislington and Redhill and the possible relocation of staff. The MD asked PTO to explore the legal side of redundancy and let the board know what payment would prove necessary.

ACTION: RQ to investigate reemployment. PTO to check redundancy provisions and payments.

6. SECURITY

The chairman voiced concern over the ease with which supermarket cans were being tampered with, especially in the US. The MD asked that a committee be set up to look at the canning process and review quality control methods.

ACTION: GD to take nominal charge of committee, choose task force, set up first meeting and report findings.

7. ANY OTHER BUSINESS

BH said she had found anomalies in the vacation time taken by two members of her staff.

ACTION: EP to draft general memo to staff on vacation responsibilities.

NEXT MEETING: Friday 7 July, 10am – 12noon. In the Boardroom.

Q

What are meetings for?

'Meetings are by definition a concession to deficient organization', writes Peter Drucker in *The Effective Executive*, 'for one either meets or one works. One cannot do both at the same time.'

Robert Townsend in *Up the Organisation* states, 'The fewer the better.'

Meetings attract abuse because they tend to be too long and too frequently held.

But the most important tasks in a business depend on people working together, cooperatively. Meetings play a vital part in making the whole business as good as the sum of its parts by:
● Reminding individuals how their hour-by-hour labours contribute to the larger corporate scheme.
● Enabling managers to be perceived as leaders rather than as officials to whom individuals report.
● Defining groups with collective aims.
● Allowing group members to exchange views.
● Promoting commitment to collective decisions.

Most important, meetings are for achieving results. Problems requiring attention can be solved on the spot by the simple act of minuting 'Action'.

Q

What are the signs of a badly conducted meeting and what can be done to make improvements?

Recognize the symptoms and the cures should be obvious. Meetings are badly conducted when:
● It's unclear from the agenda whether items are included for discussion or for making decisions.
● People who won't be affected by the outcome are invited to meetings called to decide on a course of action.
● More than six people are expected to reach a consensus.
● Some participants habitually say nothing or do no more than present information without having the power to comment.
● Requests for information are stalled until another time – this leads to further meetings.
● Decisions are taken without a specific person being designated to translate them into action by a certain time.
● The chairman leaves, or allows one of those present to leave, to take a phone call.
● It's conducted at a round table. These militate against discussion (too much space between the participants) and confuse the hierarchy.

Q

My company's numerous meetings must cost a lot of money, both in cash and management time. How can I assess the high price of these gatherings and how can it be reduced?

Think of it this way: a meeting of 10 key figures at which 15 minutes is taken up in latecoming and chitchat wastes 2 hours 30 minutes of executive time.

Work out the time spent in meetings and multiply it by the hourly salary of each participant. You'll be amazed how much company money is being spent.

To reduce costs:
● Ask your staff to cut down meeting time – frequency, duration or both – by one-third.
● Deformalize the proceedings. Instead of elaborate meetings, formally structured, slow and ponderous, which take up the whole afternoon, arrange small-scale meetings in which specific decisions are made.
● Consider adopting 'message switching' technology. Conference lines which accommodate several people on the telephone simultaneously may work out less expensive than getting everyone to stop work and go to the boardroom for 90 minutes.

Q

What is the point of a brainstorming session? Has it a place in traditional management circles?

Spontaneous discussion in search of new ideas has proved to be an invaluable management technique for finding creative solutions when normal procedures of reasoning have failed.

Brainstorming is often the last resort in the more creative purlieus of business, such as advertising and publishing: last year a British creative team stayed up all night in a plush hotel room, buoyed up by coffee and brandy, until they found a slogan for their new multi-million pound beer account.

Brainstorming has few rules, but they are essential. To work, brainstorming requires:

● An atmosphere of quasi-informality, extempore invention and mutual respect.

● That there should be no criticism of anybody's ideas, however far-fetched, expensive-sounding or obviously flawed.

● A manager to encourage the ideas to emerge.

The manager in charge should:

● Define for everyone's benefit exactly what the problem is – but no more. Explaining why no solution has yet been reached discourages participants from exploring avenues where others have failed.

● Ask each person to suggest a few ideas. They need not be detailed, finely wrought, costed out or even entirely serious, as long as they tackle the problem head on.

● Write down the ideas (in note form of course) on a blackboard or flipchart where they can be seen and mulled over for the duration of the meeting.

● Invite each contributor in turn to elaborate on his/her ideas.

● When everyone's finished (and latecoming ideas should be welcomed) steer the meeting toward assessing the ideas, tearing some to shreds and approving, for further examination, the survivors.

Q

I've been told by some friends in advertising that a course in group dynamics is a good way to prepare for confrontational meetings. Is this true?

Most of what you learn on a course in group dynamics will be useful only if the other people at your meetings have also attended one. Unless you understand the subtle rivalries that already exist between the participants, theories of group behaviour won't help.

Meetings are not arenas for winning and losing behavioural games. Issues, not people, are paramount.

Meetings are business forums where you put your point across by remorseless logic, not vicious argument.

Stifle a potentially atrabilious exchange by sticking to your guns, but show you are willing to understand the opposing view. If you describe your opponent's position as you see it and check that it's a fair summation, you can then explain why it won't work. Of course, others will do the same with your ideas.

Emotionally racked executives soon depart from logic and coherence. It doesn't take a group dynamics seminar to teach you how to capitalize on that.

Q

Now I've become departmental head I'm expected to attend a dozen meetings a month. How can I establish which ones are important?

There's a difference between important and worthwhile.

You may feel the formal get-togethers with your superiors have more to do with status than with decision making. But you can't avoid them without risking your job.

You can, however, do something about convenings with colleagues and staff. Consider the types of meeting you hold or attend and find ways of increasing their value:
● The departmental weekly gatherings. Set up, instead, a series of short one-to-one discussions.
● The weekly progress meeting. Send a lesser manager and ask him/her to report back to you.
● The eight-person, fortnightly committee meeting. Cut it down to six participants – the maximum for productive discussion – and set a time limit.
● The information gathering meeting. Ask the people involved to meet you for 10 minutes.

Alternatively, arrange for a small, non-hierarchical standing committee to be available to troubleshoot through areas of contention.

Q

At our management meetings the product research manager never says anything. How can I get him to contribute?

Does the research manager have a role to play in the meetings? Could he have assumed he's there just to soak up information? Is he biding his time until he's sure of his findings?

If he does have a function, consider his silence from a psychological point of view:
● Is he shy?
● Could he be nursing a grievance? Is his department short of money, or understaffed?
● Is it a personality clash with another participant? Does the marketing manager constantly reject suggestions emanating from the research team?

You can do something positive about this problem in five minutes. Talk to your silent colleague. Discuss his department's projects. Offer to put a special item on the agenda about product research for the next meeting.

Either he'll be pleased by your interest and the chance to justify his role; or you'll have precipitated a crisis and he'll tell you what's bothering him. Either way, you'll know where to go from there.

Q

I've just taken over as departmental manager, called my immediate staff and told them we'll have weekly meetings so that we know what everybody's doing. I'm encountering some resistance. Why?

Probably because they suspect you of calling unnecessary meetings. They are afraid their time will be wasted as you new-broom your way forward.

Your staff's work represents the co-operation (in a single unit) of some, not all, members of the department; in other words, they don't need to find out what everybody's doing.

It would be better to hold a series of smaller, informal meetings to discuss the work that directly concerns each unit of the department. Then you can determine how often you will need to meet in the future.

It pays to be specific about the reasons for a meeting and what you expect it to achieve. That way you avoid personnel-trap meetings that have all the substance and appeal of a weekly date with a barrage balloon.

Unless there is a direct reason for their presence at regular gatherings, people will quickly start going AWOL.

Q

Our meetings tend to conclude with a general discussion of points raised, and things sometimes drag on interminably. What can be done to hurry the meeting along?

If you're choosing the time of a meeting, and you want to ensure a brisk conclusion, make it fairly late in the working day – say 4.30. Within the hour, people will be thinking of trains and home and will not be disposed to linger.

If you can't do this, and no finishing time has been specified and the chairman can't be relied on to guillotine off-the-point discussion, you will need to be blunt.

If you have a power of veto, use it to bring in a crisp summing-up: 'As I see it, we have three possible lines of action/things to establish by next time/areas of responsibility to decide.' Tick them off on your fingers – numbers always lend an air of precision – and if a choice is to be made, decide on one there and then, and ask, not for views, but for votes.

It's the only way to steer the meeting toward a definite outcome. Sometimes it works; sometimes you'll be met with 'Oh come on, it isn't as simple as that.'

Q

Meetings always start late, with important people drifting in 15 to 20 minutes after the start time. What can be done?

When persuasion, bullying and cajoling fail to work, it's time to look for the root of the problem. Latecomers may feel that their presence is irrelevant; so make sure that only staff who are necessary for contributing information or for voting decisions are included.

It's more likely, however, that they object to the tedium of the open-ended meeting and attend, with reluctance, as late as possible.

The solution to this is simple. Present the meeting as occupying a clearly-defined slice of time in which decisions will be briskly reached and action initiated. Say, 'This meeting will begin at 3.15 sharp and end promptly at 4.00.' When staff relate the idea of a meeting to precision rather than flannel, they'll start turning up on the dot.

Professor C. Northcote Parkinson's solution is called 'punctuosity'. He suggests calling a meeting at, say 2.27 pm, to end on the dot of 3.51 pm. Then everyone will attend out of curiosity at such precision.

Q

Are there any guidelines about how long a meeting should last, how much time should be spent on each agenda item, and so on?

How long is a piece of string? Obviously management meetings must vary according to company, size of board and complexity of the subject under discussion.

But deadlines, however arbitrary they seem, are a vital part of good management. Meetings that last longer than two hours depress the spirit and debilitate the participants. It's much better to have two meetings with fewer people for a shorter duration.

Once you set a time scale (with a beginning and an end) you can then allot a specific period for each item. Thirty minutes on the forthcoming sales convention? Twenty minutes on the presentation from the finance director? Only the meeting's convenor can say, but say you must, and, once you decide, stick to it. Cut through waffle by asking for facts rather than subjective opinion.

Q

We've decided to rotate the chairmanship of departmental meetings, to keep them sharp. It's my turn on Friday. What should my priorities be?

Ideally, as chairman, your priority should be to avoid forcing your point of view. Your functions are primarily to:

● Expedite the proceedings.

● Stick to the agenda.

● Be brisk and ruthless about procedure.

● Cut out waffle, prejudice and digression.

● Summarize opposing points of view.

● Take a group vote on issues left undecided.

● Initiate active solutions, to be carried out by the next meeting.

You must also be something of a psychologist and see that fair play is done.

If there's a nervous new manager present, don't intimidate him/her with requests for information; let him/her try to impress you.

If there is a forthright member of the group with decided views on, say, industrial relations, and you are trying to discuss forthcoming layoffs, make a point of asking the others present for their information first, so that all the facts will be available before the debate opens.

Lastly, you must be sure that everybody at the meeting knows what they are supposed to know. Meetings are as much about the exchange of information as about discussion and decision making. Ask yourself if you are sure everyone has all the facts about the new technological gadgetry being introduced; the reason for the change in budgeting procedure; or the implications of the new government ruling.

Q

In meetings I often say too much and then regret it. How can I curb my tongue without dulling my enthusiasm?

Be more sophisticated. Childish enthusiasm won't help your arguments.

Meetings should be conducted on one level of debate – rational, serious and dispassionate. However, since human beings are involved, it is hardly surprising that, even in business, passions are raised.

The best operators at meetings are those who can act out an emotional response.

Experienced players of the meetings game are adept at losing their tempers strategically.

Don't let yourself be carried away again. Try to divorce what you say from the way you say it by deciding in advance:

● The line you wish to adopt for each item of the agenda.

● What points you need to make (write an *aide-mémoire* if necessary).

● Whether you are going to sound angry, sceptical, amused, coolly detached or apoplectic.

At the meeting, adopt your chosen tone of voice and say just what you planned to say and no more. You'll be surprised at the effect of your gamesmanship.

Q

I'm responsible for interpreting my department's monthly production when the main board meets. The rest of the agenda doesn't concern me directly. Should I excuse myself after I've spoken, or will that seem as if I'm not interested in the company's operations?

No, it won't. It will show a reluctance to waste your, and the board's, time.

If you don't belong in a discussion, say so and get out. There is work to be done elsewhere, as you of all people know. The board will appreciate your devotion to duty.

Nothing is worse than a meeting full of managers who have been invited along 'just in case'.

If you think your role in a coming meeting is likely to be marginal, don't attend. Send a memo to the chairman explaining that you don't think you'll be needed (and why) – but that all the relevant information about your current projects is in the hands of another participant.

Let it be known that you will gladly attend part of the meeting at short notice if necessary.

Q

I am the only woman in a group of seven middle managers who meet the boss for report and discussion every Wednesday. It maddens me when I am expected to take notes, yet I don't want to put everyone's back up by refusing. Now the tray with coffee and cups is being put down in front of me as if I'm supposed to be 'Mother'. How do I react?

It's possible your colleagues are just being grossly insensitive rather than deliberately rude about your status. Perhaps they feel you might be 'happier' as the coffee-dispensing stenographer.

Whatever the truth, you can't let it go on. Time for some action – but do it *sotto voce*, or you risk being stigmatized for the rest of your days.

At the start of the next meeting, have a word with the chairman and explain that you think the most junior of the executives present should be the one to take notes. Don't stand on your dignity – the chairman will understand perfectly what you mean.

If there's a general objection from the other six to the idea of taking minutes (the men having no training in secretarial skills), then move that the chairman's secretary be drafted in.

Agree to take minutes yourself only if the others each agree to do it in rotation.

As to the coffee ritual, it's a bit of role playing to which you must not rise. Act as though it's

perfectly reasonable that you should be the first to receive coffee, then show your independence by pouring a cup for yourself and passing the tray to the next person.

There's no need to explode. Just let them know that you can rise above any boorish chauvinism, because you're sure of yourself.

Q

What is the best way of getting and keeping the attention of an audience?

Audience research has proved that the average audience attends to only about one-third of a speech. Equally, analysis of human performance has shown that audiences are at their most attentive at the start of a speech, that their interest gradually falls away and that a clear indication that the speech is coming to an end brings them to life again.

All you can do about the failings of the human brain is to capitalize on them.

● Concentrate on your opening gambit and make it good. An opening phrase such as 'My subject tonight . . .' is unacceptable.

● Relax the audience with, for example, a couple of oblique but humorous remarks about your host or by recounting your embarrassing experiences at a recent similar gathering.

● Provide visual back-up. The choice is enormous, from simple flip-charts to sophisticated slide projectors.

The easiest of all the rules to remember is this: Tell the people what you're going to tell them, tell them, then tell them you've told them . . .

Q

I don't mind making a few points at a meeting, but I pale at the thought of a public presentation. How can I conquer my fear?

Few people indeed are natural orators. All the confidence and charm that exudes from most good public speakers has been learned as a management skill. You can learn it too.

When speaking at a presentation, because yours is the only voice that breaks the silence, it is impossible to ascertain what effect you're having – and your immediate response is to assume disaster.

The only way to conquer your fear is through practice. In this instance it really does make perfect.

Boost your confidence by repeating to yourself these incontrovertible truths:

● What you have to say is interesting.

● You are far from being the worst speaker you have ever heard.

● Your facts are correct.

Q

I pride myself on my speech writing. Balance, pace and content are all excellent, but I know my voice is far from perfect. Are there any exercises I can do to improve it?

Your aim is not so much to improve your voice as to sound convincing. These few rules should help you improve your delivery:

1 Make sure you pitch your voice correctly. Don't shout, but don't be too conversational. Imagine you are trying to catch the attention of someone in the back row.

2 At important moments – the punch line, the summing up, the revelation – change pitch completely. Be loud, conspiratorial . . . or whatever suits best.

3 Look around the room constantly, as if taking in every member of the audience in turn. Smile at individuals to encourage complicity.

4 Use occasional hand gestures to make you seem confident and full of conviction, but be sure not to overdo these.

Don't try out your vocal style on a tape recorder and criticize the playback. You will probably be dismayed beyond repair.

Q

I have to give a talk about the shipping industry (in which my company's involved) at a dinner next week. What's the best way to prepare for it?

Presumably you will speak direct from the high table or from a rostrum, so there is no need to worry about this aspect of presentation. If, however, you will be speaking into a microphone, be sure that this is tested well ahead of time.

Otherwise, concentrate on the script. Have a long, hard think about the subject. You cannot advertise your own company for half an hour, but are you confident or informed enough to pontificate about the entire shipping industry? In other words, how much homework should you do? Should you visit your company library or a business library to help fill the gaps in your knowledge?

Having acquired all the information you need, decide on the points you want to emphasize. Choose a certain number (say five) which will become the framework of your plan. You might, for example, start with a global overview of the shipping, freight and container markets (go easy on the statistics for a lay audience), then deal with:

● The reasons for its decline.

● Some of the geo-political factors involved.

● How certain companies (such as your own) are growing through specialization.

● An optimistic statement about the future of the world's shipping lines.

On this simple structure you can hang all manner of details, stories (true and apocryphal), case histories and so on as they occur to you over the days leading up to your speech.

When planning a speech you must be aware of the nature of your audience. Are they, for instance, businesspeople or philanthropists?

Try to work out what kind of information the audience would be interested to receive, and what sympathies they could be expected to have. You should not defer to their prejudices, but be sure you are aware of them.

Try to strike a balance between earnestness (to show you are taking the subject seriously) and levity (because you have been chosen to entertain as well as instruct).

Audiences tend, by nature, to be dull and unresponsive, so think of ways to vary your delivery and pace. Devices such as rhetorical questions ('After all, isn't peace important?'); adapted proverbs or sayings (like Prime Minister Thatcher's famous 'the lady's not for turning'); litotes (understatements); jokes and puns all help to keep the audience alert.

Finally, obey these cardinal rules of speech making:

1 When writing your speech, don't confuse the spoken and the written word. A speech that sounds like a *Times* leader will fall flat.
2 Don't be too literary, too philosophical or too grandiose.
3 Short sentences are easier to deliver than long ones, but mix the two in the interests of variety.
4 Clarity is the most important attribute of a good speech, closely followed by attractiveness of style.
5 Never read a speech from a piece of paper. Write it out on file cards, highlighting key thoughts or difficult passages with coloured marker pen. Hold the cards in your hand and refer to them discreetly.
6 Practise in front of a mirror until you're word perfect.
7 Don't talk too fast – this is the most common error of all.

Q

Is there an easy way of remembering how to organize a business memo or letter?

Help your memory with the mnemonic BRIEF. The letters stand for:

● Basics   ● Reasons   ● Initiatives   ● Expectations   ● Finishing off

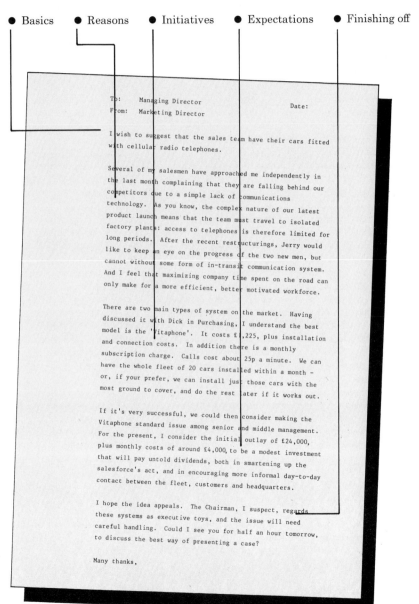

To: Managing Director   Date:
From: Marketing Director

I wish to suggest that the sales team have their cars fitted with cellular radio telephones.

Several of my salesmen have approached me independently in the last month complaining that they are falling behind our competitors due to a simple lack of communications technology. As you know, the complex nature of our latest product launch means that the team must travel to isolated factory plants: access to telephones is therefore limited for long periods. After the recent restructurings, Jerry would like to keep an eye on the progress of the two new men, but cannot without some form of in-transit communication system. And I feel that maximizing company time spent on the road can only make for a more efficient, better motivated workforce.

There are two main types of system on the market. Having discussed it with Dick in Purchasing, I understand the best model is the 'Vitaphone'. It costs £1,225, plus installation and connection costs. In addition there is a monthly subscription charge. Calls cost about 25p a minute. We can have the whole fleet of 20 cars installed within a month - or, if your prefer, we can install just those cars with the most ground to cover, and do the rest later if it works out.

If it's very successful, we could then consider making the Vitaphone standard issue among senior and middle management. For the present, I consider the initial outlay of £24,000, plus monthly costs of around £4,000, to be a modest investment that will pay untold dividends, both in smartening up the salesforce's act, and in encouraging more informal day-to-day contact between the fleet, customers and headquarters.

I hope the idea appeals. The Chairman, I suspect, regards these systems as executive toys, and the issue will need careful handling. Could I see you for half an hour tomorrow, to discuss the best way of presenting a case?

Many thanks,

Q

The five rules of the BRIEF mnemonic apply to all business communications:

● Basics. Come to the point immediately. Even if you're offering a finely argued philosophical enquiry, it's advisable to begin with your conclusions.

Suggestions, points of order, specific enquiries and outright abuse all benefit from initial bluntness.

● Reasons. After the What comes the Why. State the problem as it stands, whether it involves a sum of money or a personnel scandal.

● Initiatives. Say what you think should be done.

Demonstrate that you are an independent and efficient problem solver. Don't be too revolutionary – the recipients of your memos will invariably wish to add their own thoughts to the matter – but make your suggestion bright and apparently obvious.

● Expectations. A refinement on the above. To show you've thought the matter through, offer a forecast of how you see your plan turning out.

● Finishing off. If you're firing several memos at people with different sympathies, try to enlist their help with a (hand-written) PS. Nothing fancy – just a recognition that you remembered them specially. It pays dividends.

How do I give my written communications maximum impact?

The watchwords are clarity, simplicity, logic and brevity.

1 Make it clear from the start what kind of document you're presenting – whether minutes, a discussion paper, a memo with recommendations or a report for filing.

2 Factual documents and reports, covering several areas of enquiry, should be given a detailed 'Contents' section.

3 Lay it out in clear sections, with underlined headings, titles and subtitles. That way, your readers can easily identify the parts that concern them most.

4 Keep your sentences short, punchy and to the point. Avoid circumlocution, jargon and foreign tags.

5 Go easy on punctuation – never use a semi-colon where a full stop would suffice.

6 Paragraphs are units of thought, not slabs of prose. Keep them short. Remember the average person's attention span is generally no more than 150 words in unbroken sequence.

7 Avoid generalizations. You're presumably arguing a point, trying to persuade or seeking an effect. You'll do that best through sticking to the facts and expressing them with flair.

8 What's the final point of your communication? Set out your conclusions clearly and obviously. A busy colleague or boss is likely to skip your clever reasoning and read the conclusions first.

Persuasion and negotiation **86–7** *Handling your boss* **90–1**

Q

I talk well but I panic when I have to write things down. How can I learn to write with confidence?

How necessary is writing? Don't give up the sort of verbal communication you're best at unless you need to:

● Provide a permanent, unambiguous record (as in a report or contract).

● Prove that you've taken action.

● Emphasize your views.

● Supply the same information to several people.

If you have to write:

● First, think through what you need to say, and what you want to achieve, without worrying how you'll write it. Then make notes or dictate the salient points into a tape recorder.

● Write down the conclusion or key point in your argument.

● Organize the evidence for your conclusion or key point. It can be factual (eg a deadline must be met) or psychological (eg I feel that he does not fit into the team).

● Jot down the points, writing each on a separate piece of paper.

● Staple them into a logical order; you'll see at a glance how a little rewording may make points enhance their neighbours.

● You've done the work! Now follow the old preacher's adage: 'Tell the people what you're going to tell them, tell them, then tell them what you've told them.' That is, make your statement, explain it, restate it.

● Read and delete repetitious thoughts and words – they're boring. And take care the spelling and typing of the final document are accurate: a reader whose name is spelled wrongly is predisposed to disagree with you.

(Of course, on a cool reading of your final draft, you may find the evidence doesn't justify the conclusion. But that's another story.)

Q

I know my writing is fussy and over-complicated. How can I improve my style?

The key to clear writing is clear thinking. So think out what you have to say, then say it as simply as you can. Get used to polishing and rewriting until you've got the result you want. Keep in mind George Orwell's maxim that 'A scrupulous writer in every sentence that he writes, will ask himself at least four questions, thus: What am I trying to say? What words will express it? What image or idiom will make it clearer? Is this image fresh enough to have an effect?'

Orwell also laid down six ground rules for improving the quality and clarity of all written communications:

1 Never use a metaphor, simile or other figure of speech which you are used to seeing in print.

2 Never use a long word where a short one will do.

3 If it is possible to cut out a word, always cut it out.

4 Never use the passive where you can use the active.

5 Never use a foreign phrase, a scientific word or a jargon word if you can think of an everyday English equivalent.

6 Break any of these rules sooner than say anything outright barbarous.

Q

The letters I dictate to my secretary are never clear and correct first time. How can I communicate better?

Is dictation really the best method for you? If the words come out better by writing rather than saying them, why not write letters out in longhand for your secretary to type, or work them directly on to the typewriter or word processor. Your secretary can then 'top and tail' and neat-type them. Given the right information, a good secretary should be able to draft straightforward letters for you.

If you want to be a better dictator:

● Don't dictate 'cold' then leave the secretary to sort out the mess afterward.

● Practise with the dictating machine. Get used to verbalizing the expressions that give your letters bite and impact.

● Plan complicated or difficult letters before you dictate them. Make notes.

● Ask your secretary to read back what you've said immediately. Polish it up if necessary.

Q

Some of the letters and documents I receive are incomprehensible. How can I find out if the ones I write are equally obscure?

To work out the obscurity index of a piece of writing:

1 Count the number of words.

2 Count the number of sentences.

3 Divide the number of sentences by the number of words to get the average number of words per sentence.

4 Count the number of words with more than two syllables.

5 Add the results of 3 and 4.

6 Multiply the result by 0.4.

An answer of 1 or less indicates a clearly written communication. An answer of 13 or more indicates that your writing is too obscure. Try analyzing the obscurity rating of a badly written letter:

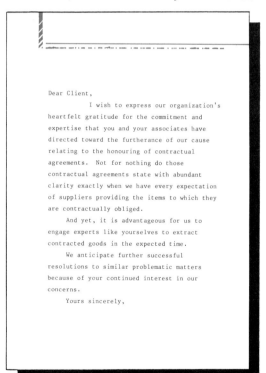

Dear Client,

I wish to express our organization's heartfelt gratitude for the commitment and expertise that you and your associates have directed toward the furtherance of our cause relating to the honouring of contractual agreements. Not for nothing do those contractual agreements state with abundant clarity exactly when we have every expectation of suppliers providing the items to which they are contractually obliged.

And yet, it is advantageous for us to engage experts like yourselves to extract contracted goods in the expected time.

We anticipate further successful resolutions to similar problematic matters because of your continued interest in our concerns.

Yours sincerely,

Obscurity rating: 26.8

There is a clearer way of saying 'Thank you for helping us to get our suppliers to deliver on time.'

Q

I feel I ought to entertain clients at the best restaurants, but I'm not confident about smart places and ordering food and drink. How do I build up my social skills?

First of all remember that luncheons for clients – however succulent the food and mellow the wine – are more than gastronomic treats. They're the backdrop to serious (though of course informal) business negotiations or vital exchanges of information. Everything else is secondary.

The best restaurants tend to be the most expensive ones. If you're entertaining an important supplier, a new and lucrative account holder, or an epicurean associate from abroad, this is fine – take them to a top-flight, multi-starred establishment. But with everyday associates and run-of-the-mill clients, spending inordinate amounts on lunch is extravagant and inappropriate. Have you nothing better to do with the company's money?

The best way to accustom yourself to lunching clients is to select a restaurant near your place of work – such as an Italian trattoria – where there is a friendly atmosphere and no posturing by the wine waiter. Cultivate it assiduously until it feels like a second home, and you are greeted by name. To begin with, take a friend or colleague and ask the waiters to explain the menu. Arrange to have the same table but order a different dish each time. Order and try the house wine before you experiment with other suggestions on the wine list.

Once you're more confident about ordering and you've mastered the art of interspersing eating with talking and listening over a two-hour period, branch out by trying some smart French or international restaurants. Try those attached to the best hotels – some of them offer set (table d'hôte) lunches at reasonable prices. If you have the set menu your guest will follow, thus avoiding the embarrassment of choice when you order à la carte.

If you're uncertain about table manners, watch your guests to see how they proceed.

Above all, learn to relax . . .

Q

I'm obliged to lunch with clients several times a week. Work is impossible afterward. What can I do to improve my afternoon performance?

Nothing could be less businesslike than allowing lunch to render you inefficient and unproductive for half the working day. This is the path to redundancy and/or cirrhosis.

Unless you're used to drinking alcohol at lunchtime, a couple of glasses of wine could make you lethargic.

Simple abstinence is the only answer. Offer your guest aperitifs and wine but don't order a full bottle and expect him or her to drink it all. Better to say, 'Would you like a glass of wine?' They'll ask if you intend to have one and you demur in favour of mineral water. Blame a heavy night or a late work session to come, but don't weaken.

Encourage your guests to order whatever they like but avoid anything too filling for yourself. Just after the main course is the time when most serious lunchtime work is accomplished – don't let distractions from the sweet trolley get in the way. If you, as host, go straight on to coffee, your guest will probably follow suit.

Q

We spend a considerable amount of time having office parties. They're good for morale but, as the company grows, so do the anniversaries. Where do I draw the line?

Office parties are undoubtedly good for morale but they can become too much of a good thing. Staff tire of the endless requests for signatures on greeting cards and contributions toward gifts.

So it's as well to have a coherent strategy about in-house jollifications. Here are a few guidelines.

● Events which affect the company are worth celebrating. A successful contract/new account/half-yearly figures or similar commercial triumph justifies a party and gives the staff a sense of being crucial to its achievement.

● Departing personnel deserve formal recognition of their contribution, but only if they have been employed for a certain time – say two years. Less than that, and it should be left to their colleagues to organize a farewell celebration.

● Christmas is a natural excuse for a party and is a good way to recharge interpersonal batteries before the New Year.

● On the other hand, birthdays are personal occasions and do not merit the spending of company money. A good manager, however, will give a secretary or a close colleague a card and a small gift.

● Weddings and engagements likewise, should be treated as occasions for the staff to make their own arrangements, although a telemessage at the reception saying 'Good luck from all your friends at the office' will be appreciated.

● Promotions and new arrivals are not occasions for parties because it remains to be seen how well the new incumbent will perform.

The personal touch need not be ignored completely, however, when occasions such as birthdays and anniversaries roll around. Staff like to think there are traditions in their company and that their Big Days can be shared. They'll happily abide by what they think is standard practice.

So why not institute a 'new tradition': dictate that the birthday boy or girl, rather than receive gifts from the staff, must buy cream cakes for everyone in the building at teatime. This approach has the additional advantage of discouraging the less generous from making too much fuss about their anniversaries.

Q

I have been invited to attend a new product launch in a seaside hotel. Should I dress to suit: (a) the company I work for (sober); (b) the product (flamboyant); or (c) the hotel (casual)?

Dress to suit the occasion: a compromise between (a) and (b). Never dress to suit an hotel: hotels exist for your comfort, not to dictate fashion.

Product launches are formal company occasions on which a lot of money will be riding. They are not parties and do not call for party dress. For male senior management, suits are *de rigueur* – dark worsted in winter months, light cotton in summer.

That apart, you can afford to be flexible. If the launch is a jaunty outdoor affair, nothing will be gained by looking like a bank manager. Lighten the formality of your suit by wearing a pastel shirt or a bow tie. Don't overdo it: even if the product is a surfboard.

Women needn't be rigidly formal but, like the men, their watchword should be 'appropriate': keep it subtle.

Above all, never do, wear, arrange or say anything that might embarrass your guests, your company or (especially) yourself.

Q

I seem to spend a great deal of time on the telephone and always hang up feeling vaguely dissatisfied. How does one cut through the waffle?

Getting to the point is the most important element in using the telephone.

There's only one way to do so: write down the information you require, or wish to convey, under the telephonee's name. When you've got the answer, or passed on the data, immediately draw a line under it.

Thereafter, anything you say or write down will be superfluous to the purpose of your call. Chat away if you please, ask anything you like, gossip to your heart's content – just as long as you know the meter's now in 'excess period'.

Cutting through other people's waffle takes skill and chutzpah. Skill is needed to get out of playing the 'How are you?/Long time no see/How's the wife and kids?/Have a nice holiday/I hear you're moving house/Did you hear about Kelly?' dialogue. It takes chutzpah to steer them gently but firmly into saying what they want and then going away.

You occasionally hear of people capable of saying, 'Could you please come to the point?' but that form of directness is a little too brusque for most people.

'What can I do for you?' is still the most tactful way of getting down to business after the 'Hellos'. If it elicits no definite response, try saying (assuming you know the caller), 'I expect you're ringing about the . . .' and refer back to the last dealings you had. If you are lucky, the caller will say 'No, actually, it's about the . . .'; if you're unlucky, you'll get a potted history of the earlier campaign thrown in as well.

Varying degrees of directness can be tried. One of my favourite *New Yorker* cartoons shows an irascible businessman answering the phone with: 'This is not an answering machine. When I go "Beep", state your business.'

Q

Some of my phone calls go on too long. How do I hang up without being rude?

Ending phone calls takes diplomacy. Some people with armour-plated skin can ignore the most obvious signs. Today's managers should be more subtle.

Here are the accredited phrases that mean 'I am going to hang up in a minute':

● 'Before I go, what happened to . . .'
● 'Well listen – very nice to hear from you again . . .'
● 'One last thing . . .'
● 'Look, we must get together soon . . .'

Disposing of people you really don't want to talk to at all takes effort. Tell them you can't talk now, because you've got a roomful of people (for some reason this always sounds plausible, no matter who says it) but will call back; then call back during the lunch break and leave a message that you rang. It'll buy you a day's grace in which to work out a more considered response.

Q

What do I do if the telephone rings while I'm having a serious talk with a colleague?

It's tempting to take the call you spent the morning waiting for, even though a colleague is with you. A brief interruption won't be intrusive, surely? Oh yes it will.

Generally speaking, people resent phone calls in the middle of a semi-formal conversation. They feel subconsciously that they and their problems, their departmental standing or their time, aren't sufficiently important to preclude interruptions. They can do nothing but twiddle their thumbs and seethe at the unseen interloper. They'll reply to your 'Now where were we?' with rancour.

Mark McCormack, the sporting-celebrity marketeer, recalls the time Spiro Agnew rang him when he was in a meeting with the editor of *Playboy* at the latter's office (he'd passed the number on to Agnew's secretary).

'Although the call had nothing to do with the business at hand,' recalls McCormack, 'our meeting took on a whole new aura of importance.' How much more impressive it would have been for McCormack to say 'Tell him I'll ring back.'

Q

I become extremely annoyed when I ring people and am told they will ring me back some time. After six of these I'm afraid to leave the office because of all the calls that are due – half of which never get returned. Calling back people who are out is equally maddening. What can be done?

Set up a more efficient message system.

Don't just leave a message to say you called and ask for the person to get back to you. Instead:

● If it's urgent, say so.
● Specify the order or the project.
● Ask for a time when he/she will be in and for your call to be returned at a specific time.

When other people call you, ask the person who answers the phone in your absence to write down the caller's name and company and the nature of the call – and to say when you will be in.

Some people use the ring-you-back syndrome as a reflex action. If you're told someone is 'in a meeting', and you're sure he is not, say quickly, 'Tell him it's Chris at Unilever and I need a one-sentence reply to a simple question.' Then it's up to the secretary. If it's a bona fide meeting, no amount of persuasion will get you through. Otherwise, such directness may work.

Q

Is it worth spending money on in-car telephones?

Car telephones, enabling you to dial direct to contacts within a limited communications 'ring', have been around for a decade.

The most sophisticated form of car phone is the cellular radiophone, so named because it works through a honeycomb of overlapping sonic cells spread across the country. Wherever you happen to be and however far you drive, the signal remains at constant strength, and you can converse with people in all major urban areas.

Are they worth spending money on? Add to the cost of buying the phones, connection and installation fees, yearly subscription and the cost of the calls per minute. They certainly aren't cheap. On the plus side, they do mean you can keep in touch with headquarters, on-the-road staff and important clients 24 hours a day.

There are also safety factors to be considered. A telephone conversation prevents you from concentrating fully on your driving. So pull over to the side of the road before making that important call.

Q

What information is a company legally bound to disclose?

The Companies Act requires every company to submit a set of annual financial statements. They must include:
● A Balance Sheet showing the company's assets and liabilities at the end of the accounting period.
● A Profit and Loss Account showing the profit or loss made during the same period.
● The comparative figures from the previous year's accounting period.
● Notes to explain certain items in the Balance Sheet and the Profit and Loss Account.
● A 'Source and Application of Funds' statement if the company's turnover, or gross income, exceeds £25,000.
● A report by the directors giving certain other information concerning, for example, directors and major shareholders, employees and information about the progress of the company (this is usually detailed in the Chairman's Statement and Review of Activities).
● The report of a qualified accountant who has subjected the accounts to an independent audit.

Q

I want to know whether the company I've been offered a job with is performing well. I've got their last annual report. What do I look for?

You need to infer a great deal from the information provided in company reports.
1 The obvious starting point is the Profit and Loss Account, which measures the current operating performance of the business and shows turnover and expenses. The pre-tax profit figure is an important pointer to overall company efficiency.
2 But a company with large profits can still collapse overnight if it lacks sufficient funds. So turn to the Balance Sheet to see how much cash is invested in the business, how the assets are balanced with liabilities and how the company is otherwise funded.
3 Look at the Source and Application of Funds, to identify the sources of the company's funds and how it spends its money: its acquisitions of other companies or increased stock, its shedding of plant or personnel.
4 Read the Chairman's Statement and Review of Activities, bearing in mind that the positive aspects will be heavily emphasized. It will tell you the company's objectives, its current success in certain markets, and (some of) its future plans. You should be able to assess how far,

and how fast, the company is growing.
5 Evaluate the performance graphs from the last few years. Do they show consistent, or increasing earnings? If necessary, obtain copies of previous annual reports and draw your own performance graphs.
6 Compare the company's graphs and figures with those of competitors.
7 Ask around.

Q

Who uses all the detailed information contained in company reports – and why are they so elaborately produced?

Company reports are not intended to help the company's own management run the business; most of the financial information will have been seen by them already. Reports are more generally used as a many-headed public relations exercise, to present the company in the best and most positive light:
● To demonstrate to shareholders that the business is thriving, and that their investment is safe and producing a reasonable return.
● To attract potential shareholders by showing that their investment would be put to the best possible use.
● To provide lending institutions with information about the company's past and present performance, to enable them to decide if the company is a worthwhile lending proposition.
  Company reports are also aimed at:
● Staff. The chairman's report may be used to convey company philosophy or describe how some major change will affect work in the future. Many companies produce a separate Employee Report for their employees' interest.
● Potential customers who wish to know how the company is faring, especially if considering placing a large order.
● Suppliers, current or potential, who will be interested in the company's ability to meet short-term financial obligations.

Q

Whenever accounts are discussed, the phrase 'true and fair view' crops up. How true is 'true'? How fair is 'fair'?

Whole books have been written attempting to define the phrase, but it remains elusive. It's a statutory requirement without a definition.
  Nonetheless, certain general principles come under the heading of 'true and fair':
● The accounts must give a *realistic* picture of the business. Nothing must be left out and nothing 'extra' put in.
● The concept of 'materiality' applies here. For example, omitting an amount of £2,000 would be considered negligible in a multi-million pound business but wholly material to a £30,000 turnover in a small firm.
● The accounts must be prepared according to generally accepted principles: those laid down by the professional accounting bodies.
● Comparative figures from previous years must be prepared on the same basis as those for the current year.
  Seeing that the figures are 'true and fair' is a responsibility of the directors; the auditors are obliged, if their findings are not satisfactory, to give an appropriately qualified report.

Profit and growth **156–7**

Q

How can I use our company's published accounts to measure its performance?

Examining the bald figures won't tell you much. You must be able to analyze and interpret what the accounts disclose. To do so, use 'ratio analysis'. This means comparing, or showing the relationship between, two sets of figures. Subsequent interpretation depends on whichever analytical system you favour. The health of your company can be judged by comparing ratios with other companies and other years.

Ratios are expressed either as percentages or

Measures of liquidity

The Current Ratio
This is the best-known indicator of a company's short-term liquidity, namely its ability to pay its debts as they fall due.

Current assets: £22,525
Current liabilities: £19,476
Ratio: 1.15:1

The greater the degree by which current assets exceed current liabilities, the more liquid the company.

The Acid Test
This ratio (also known as the Quick Ratio) assesses a company's ability to pay its debts at short notice – should its stock, for example, prove difficult to realize in a hurry.

Liquid assets (ie current assets, less stock): £10,214
Current liabilities: £19,476

Ratio: $\dfrac{10,214}{19,476} = 0.52$

Because stock can represent such a large part of a company's assets, its Quick Ratio is commonly less than 1.

Debtors to Sales
This ratio indicates the period of credit given to customers and is measured in days.

Debtors: £9,535
Sales: £51,211

Ratio: $\dfrac{9,535}{51,211} \times 365 = \dfrac{67.9 \text{ days}}{\text{credit given}}$

This ratio should be examined in the light of the prevailing credit terms for the industry. Standard business terms often lay down 30 days' credit as normal. If that's the case with your company and its ratio is over 40, your credit control needs improvement.

Suppliers to Purchase Ratio
The ratio of current trade suppliers to the value of goods purchased from them is also expressed in days. It discloses the average period of credit taken from suppliers. The figures for purchases may not always be available.

$\dfrac{\text{Trade suppliers}}{\text{Purchases}} \times 365$
= Suppliers to Purchases Ratio

Many businesses finance their operating assets by taking extended credit from suppliers, as would be shown by a higher ratio. This may damage the company's relationship with its suppliers.

---

as the number of times one figure divides into another. They are calculated from only two figures, be they stock value against turnover, or sales revenue against amounts of money owed.

Ratios are useful for measuring a company's liquidity (ability to meet its debts) and its profitability. While they rarely provide conclusive answers, they are important indicators of current trends.

The figures used below are taken from the financial statements on pages 132–5.

Measures of profitability

Return on Capital Employed
This ratio reveals whether the company is using its funds as effectively as it should and whether other companies in the same industry are making better use of their capital.

$$\frac{\text{Net profit}}{\text{Capital employed}} \times 100 \qquad = \frac{4,020}{8,095} \times 100 = 49\%$$

Net profit is shown in the Profit and Loss Account and is usually assessed as pre-tax profit. The capital employed takes the form of shareholders' funds and large-scale borrowing.

Gross Profit to Turnover
This is known as the Profit Margin Ratio. Rates of gross profit vary widely from business to business.

Gross profit: £19,044
Sales: £51,211

Ratio: $\dfrac{19,044}{51,211} \times 100 = 37\%$

Net Pre-tax Profit to Turnover
(Net profit margin)
This percentage, together with the ratio of individual costs to sales, may indicate areas for cost controls etc.

Net profit: £4,020
Turnover: £51,211

Ratio: $\dfrac{4,020}{51,211} \times 100 = 7.8\%$

Q

What can I learn about our company from the Balance Sheet?

Not as much as you may think. The Balance Sheet only gives what amounts to a 'snapshot' of the company's financial position at a certain date.

Several of the figures given in the Balance Sheet are further analyzed in the 'Notes', which appear farther on in the accounts.

1 A Balance Sheet is basically a statement of what a company owns

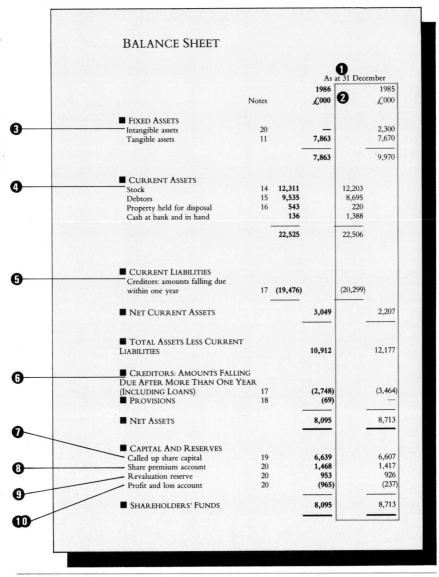

BALANCE SHEET

	Notes	1986 £000	1985 £000
❶ As at 31 December ❷			
■ **FIXED ASSETS** ❸			
Intangible assets	20	—	2,300
Tangible assets	11	**7,863**	7,670
		7,863	9,970
■ **CURRENT ASSETS** ❹			
Stock	14	**12,311**	12,203
Debtors	15	**9,535**	8,695
Property held for disposal	16	**543**	220
Cash at bank and in hand		**136**	1,388
		22,525	22,506
■ **CURRENT LIABILITIES** ❺			
Creditors: amounts falling due within one year	17	**(19,476)**	(20,299)
■ **NET CURRENT ASSETS**		**3,049**	2,207
■ **TOTAL ASSETS LESS CURRENT LIABILITIES**		**10,912**	12,177
■ **CREDITORS: AMOUNTS FALLING DUE AFTER MORE THAN ONE YEAR (INCLUDING LOANS)** ❻	17	**(2,748)**	(3,464)
■ **PROVISIONS**	18	**(69)**	—
■ **NET ASSETS**		**8,095**	8,713
■ **CAPITAL AND RESERVES** ❼			
Called up share capital	19	**6,639**	6,607
Share premium account ❽	20	**1,468**	1,417
Revaluation reserve ❾	20	**953**	926
Profit and loss account	20	**(965)**	(237)
■ **SHAREHOLDERS' FUNDS** ❿		**8,095**	8,713

(assets) and what it owes (liabilities) at a particular date.

2 Figures are also given for the end of the previous accounting period, so you can see if the company's position has improved or deteriorated.

3 Fixed assets tie up company money on a long-term basis. They are divided into 'tangible' and 'intangible' assets.

Tangible assets tend to be such items as land and buildings, plant and machinery – the actual hardware used to operate the business.

Intangible assets are such things as goodwill, patents and licences.

4 Current assets are those which can be readily converted into cash (ie within one year): stock, debtors and cash.

5 Current liabilities are debts which are due for payment in less than a year – for example, bank overdrafts and payment to suppliers.

6 Longer-term liabilities are those that need not be repaid for more than one year. They may include bank loans and mortgages.

7 Called up share capital represents the number of shares the company has issued. If the company were to cease trading, any money left after settling liabilities would

be distributed proportionately among the shareholders.

8 The share premium account represents the difference between the nominal value of a company's shares and the actual price at which they are issued.

Usually this price is the same as the 'par', or nominal value, of the shares when they are first issued on the formation of the company. But if a company has been trading successfully for some time, its shares will be worth more than their nominal value, and so they are issued at a premium to that value.

9 When assets such as freehold land are valued, their value may be greater than the original cost. The difference between these two figures is included as *revaluation reserve*, to show it is not a profit which the company has realized in cash terms, and that it cannot be distributed to shareholders.

10 The Profit and Loss Account figure represents the profits the company has earned, in previous years as well as in the current year, along with any other distributable reserves which have not been distributed as a dividend to shareholders.

The Balance Sheet gives a view of the company at only a single point in time. The company's position may be markedly different soon after that date (although any significant post-Balance Sheet events should be recorded in the accounts' 'Stop Press').

The net assets figure does not represent the real market value of the company's assets. The figures are based on what the assets cost to buy; they don't reveal resale or replacement value.

As a result, although the company may appear to be making a good return on assets, those assets may soon need replacing – at a cost far greater than that shown.

The Balance Sheet mixes assets and liabilities that have been bought with pounds of different purchasing power. For example, an asset costing £100 five years ago has the same cost figure in the accounts as an asset costing £100 one week ago.

Because the Balance Sheet is concerned only with matters that can be expressed in financial terms, it does not cover such items as labour relations, market position, management resources or growth of the industry in which the company is involved.

Q

How does the Profit and Loss Account measure the operating performance of a business?

By displaying the business's turnover, or sales revenue, alongside the cost of goods sold, and other expenses, over a period of time – usually a year.

1 The sales turnover figure shows the total sales made by the company during the period. Elsewhere in the accounts (in the Notes), it will be further analyzed, by class of business and

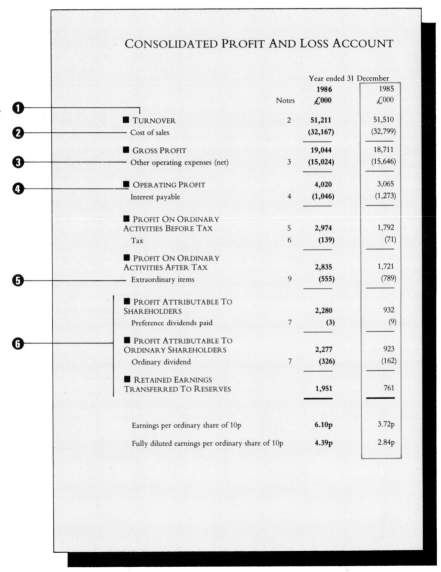

CONSOLIDATED PROFIT AND LOSS ACCOUNT

	Notes	Year ended 31 December 1986 £000	1985 £000
■ TURNOVER	2	51,211	51,510
Cost of sales		(32,167)	(32,799)
■ GROSS PROFIT		19,044	18,711
Other operating expenses (net)	3	(15,024)	(15,646)
■ OPERATING PROFIT		4,020	3,065
Interest payable	4	(1,046)	(1,273)
■ PROFIT ON ORDINARY ACTIVITIES BEFORE TAX	5	2,974	1,792
Tax	6	(139)	(71)
■ PROFIT ON ORDINARY ACTIVITIES AFTER TAX		2,835	1,721
Extraordinary items	9	(555)	(789)
■ PROFIT ATTRIBUTABLE TO SHAREHOLDERS		2,280	932
Preference dividends paid	7	(3)	(9)
■ PROFIT ATTRIBUTABLE TO ORDINARY SHAREHOLDERS		2,277	923
Ordinary dividend	7	(326)	(162)
■ RETAINED EARNINGS TRANSFERRED TO RESERVES		1,951	761
Earnings per ordinary share of 10p		6.10p	3.72p
Fully diluted earnings per ordinary share of 10p		4.39p	2.84p

❶ ❷ ❸ ❹ ❺ ❻

geographical region.

2 Cost of sales is the cost directly attributable to sales of the company's goods or services, for example, the cost of raw materials, factory heating and lighting. Deducting the cost-of-sales figure from turnover gives the gross profit.

3 Other operating expenses include all costs the company incurs in its everyday trading operations, such as the sales force's car bills and office administration costs. Deducting this figure from the gross profit gives the trading, or operating, profit.

4 This section covers items which are part of the company's activities, but are not a direct part of its trading operation: for example, the income from the company's investments.

5 Extraordinary items are amounts relating to material events outside the normal activities of the business which are not expected to recur.

6 The profit that remains is partly allocated to shareholders in the form of a dividend – in effect, the 'interest' they have earned on their investment – and partly retained by the business to finance its continuing operations.

Q

How is it that a company's taxation figure can change so dramatically from year to year, even though the profits are similar?

Calculating how much a company should pay in tax can be extremely complicated. Although it may have earned a profit in the year, it may pay little tax if it made losses in previous years.

The tax bill may also be small if the company has allowances for expenditure incurred on fixed assets which are not the same as the amounts by which those assets were depreciated, or 'written down', in the accounts.

Q

How are earnings per share calculated, and what are they used for?

Earnings are calculated by dividing the year's profits (before any extraordinary items but after preference dividends) by the number of shares issued. It indicates the total earnings – dividends and the amounts retained for expansion – which each share has generated during the year.

If a company has granted options to subscribe for its shares at some future date, the 'fully diluted' earnings per share will be given, showing what effect the conversion of these options into shares would have.

The earnings-per-share figure tends to influence the market value of the shares. For companies which have their shares listed on the Stock Exchange, a 'price earnings ratio' (the relationship between earnings per share and current market value per share) is printed daily in the financial press.

Evaluating your assets **140–1** *Profit and growth* **156–7**

Q

What can I learn from the Statement of Source and Application of Funds?

The SSAF is often a better guide to a company's health than either the Profit and Loss Account or the Balance Sheet.

It gives answers to the following questions:
● Are normal company operations generating sufficient funds to enable it to continue in business, or is the company having to fund itself through increased borrowing/sales of assets/issue of shares?
● How is the company using the funds it generates, and is it using them wisely?

Q

How can a company be earning profits but still be short of cash?

There could be several reasons; an examination of the SSAF should help pinpoint the main ones. A company may:
● Be selling on deferred terms, so that it must pay its suppliers before it receives payment from its customers – thus putting a strain on its cash flow.
● Have been operating with old plant and machinery, and so charging low depreciation to the Profit and Loss Account. When it has to replace that machinery, it may strain its cash resources.
● Have repaid loans for which insufficient cash was generated.
● Be overtrading or under-capitalized – that is, the company does not have sufficient working capital to fund its operations when demand becomes unusually high.
● Not have retained sufficient funds to pay previous years' tax bills; tax falls due several months after a company's year end, and it can take years to agree how much tax a company owes.

Q

How does the Statement of Source and Application of Funds show changes in the company's financial position?

All companies with a turnover, or gross profit, of more than £25,000 are required to prepare a statement itemizing where the company's funds have come from and how they have been used.
1 A company's main source of funds is usually trading profit. It must be able to generate enough internal resources; otherwise it can't survive. Other sources include sales of fixed assets, long-term borrowing or a new issue of shares.
2 Certain items, such as depreciation of fixed assets used in the business, must be 'added back' to profit. That is to say, assets, whose value has decreased because they were used in the business, have reduced the profit by the amount of this decrease. Although they are costs which are charged against profit, they are not cash items, so the profit figure has to be adjusted to show the 'cash profit'.
3 Funds are applied or used to:
● Pay dividends to shareholders.
● Invest in other companies.

STATEMENT OF SOURCE AND APPLICATION OF FUNDS

	Year ended 31 December			
	1986		1985	
	£000		£000	
■ SOURCE OF FUNDS				
Profit on ordinary activities before tax	**2,974**		1,792	
Items not involving the movement of funds:				
Depreciation and amounts written off fixed assets	**798**		903	
FUNDS GENERATED FROM OPERATIONS	**3,772**		2,695	
Proceeds of sale of subsidiaries and businesses*	**1,046**		2,292	
Proceeds of sale of tangible fixed assets	**409**		226	
Share issue	**83**		43	
Tax repaid	**19**		—	
		1,557		2,561
TOTAL SOURCE OF FUNDS	**5,329**		5,256	
■ APPLICATION OF FUNDS				
Goodwill written off	**(207)**		(53)	
Extraordinary items	**(445)**		(789)	
Purchase of tangible fixed assets	**(2,356)**		(1,598)	
Dividends paid	**(256)**			
Bank loans repaid	**(715)**		(780)	
TOTAL APPLICATION OF FUNDS		**(3,979)**		(3,220)
NET SOURCE OF FUNDS	**1,350**		2,036	
THE NET SOURCE OF FUNDS IS REPRESENTED BY THE FOLLOWING INCREASE (DECREASE) IN WORKING CAPITAL:				
Stock	**788**		1,568	
Debtors	**840**		1,447	
Property held for disposal	**(220)**		(217)	
Creditors	**211**		(2,703)	
		1,619		95
Movements in net liquid funds:				
(Increase)/decrease in net bank overdrafts		**(269)**		1,941
		1,350		2,036

*SALE OF SUBSIDIARIES AND BUSINESSES

ASSETS SOLD	£000
Fixed assets	366
Stock	680
Proceeds of sale	1,046

● Repay a long-term debt.
● Buy new fixed assets.
● Go toward paying taxes.
4 Working capital may be seen to increase or decrease. An increase may result if more cash than usual has been tied up in stocks or in debtors. On the other hand, stock purchases may have been funded only at the expense of increasing creditors.

Q

There are numerous words our finance director uses when discussing company accounts that are never defined. Can you help?

Accruals
A fundamental concept in the preparation of accounts. It means that income or costs are allowed for when they are incurred and not when the cash is either received or paid out.

Amortization
The writing off, over a period of time, of an asset or a debt. It's customary to amortize the cost of, say, development costs by charging instalments of the lump sum paid against the company's profits each year.

Asset
An asset is something you own or have use of. Items used in the business, such as plant and machinery, are known as fixed assets. Current assets are those which can readily be converted into cash.

Debenture
Strictly, a document which sets out the terms of a loan raised on the security of a property which the lender can sell if the borrower defaults on payments. The best known form of debenture is a mortgage.

Goodwill
A specific term meaning more than reputation, it is the amount paid for something over and above the value of its constituent parts or the value shown in the seller's accounts. It is usually the difference between the asset worth of a company and its value on the open market.

Liability
Liabilities are sums owed by a company to someone else. Long-term liabilities are those not due for repayment within a year; current ones are those due within the year.

Liabilities may be 'deferred' for longer periods by arrangement with the creditor.

Subsidiary company
A company is a subsidiary of another if that other company controls the composition of its board of directors and holds more than half the nominal value of its equity share capital, or is already a subsidiary of another company which is a subsidiary of the first company.

Minority interests
If a company has a subsidiary of which it does not own all the shares, the other shareholders are collectively known as 'the minority'. Their share of the profits or losses, and the assets of that subsidiary will be shown in the Profit and Loss Account and the Balance Sheet.

Associate company
An associate company is usually defined as one which is more than 20% owned by another company, which exercises a significant degree of management control. That company will then take on to the Profit and Loss Account its share of the associate's profits or losses.

Q

How do ordinary shares differ from other kinds?
What changes can a company make to its share
capital and in what markets can the shares be traded?

Ordinary shares

An ordinary share gives
the holder the right to
participate in the profits
of a company and also the
right to vote on major
decisions affecting the
company.

Preference shares

A preference share
carries the right to a fixed
rate of dividend before
any dividends are paid to
ordinary shareholders; it
will also have fixed
repayment terms. It gives
greater security than an
ordinary share, but
forgos any rewards of
high growth. It may also
carry the right to convert
into an ordinary share.

Consolidation of shares

A company's shares are
consolidated when their
nominal value is raised
by declaring that,
'Henceforth, every 20 five
pence shares shall be one
£1.00 share.' The opposite
process (the subdividing
of share capital) is
another option.

Deferred shares

These carry no right to a
dividend. The idea is that
their owners will
participate later in the
capital growth of the
company.

Rights issue

This gives a company's
shareholders the
opportunity to invest
more money in the
company by subscribing
for new shares at a cost
which is less than the
current market price. The
issue is made on the basis
of, for example, one new
share for every two held.

Bonus/scrip issue

Shareholders are given
more shares without
having to make a direct
payment. The company
effectively pays for them
itself by using some of the
reserves it has built up.
The free issue of shares
has the aim of increasing
the number of
shareholders and the
marketability of the
shares.

Main market

Every country has a
principal Stock
Exchange, on which
shares of larger
companies are traded.
These companies can be
both domestic and
foreign.

Secondary market

Many countries also have
secondary markets for
smaller companies, with
less stringent admission
requirements, eg the
Unlisted Securities
Market in the UK. Often,
expanding companies
transfer in time from the
secondary to the primary
market.

Other markets

Some companies may be
able to sell their shares to
the public through a
dealer in securities, who
will himself make a
market in those shares,
matching potential
buyers and sellers. A
more formal development
of this exists in the 'Over
the Counter' market,
operated by the larger
licensed dealers.

Equity and ownership **154–5**   *Profit and growth* **156–7**

Q

How do companies assess the value of the stock in their warehouses?

They may use one of three common methods:
1 FIFO – First In, First Out. This means that articles are taken out of stock (financially speaking) in the order in which they were purchased. The year-end stock valuation is, therefore, based on the cost of the most recent purchases.

With this method, product cost tends to be lower, and stock value higher, than with other methods.
2 LIFO – Last In, First Out. This means that articles are taken out of stock at the most recent purchase price. Stock valuation is, therefore, based on the oldest purchase costs for the period.
3 Average – by this method, stock is valued at the average purchase cost for the period.

Q

What exactly is being evaluated when accountants talk about the 'depreciation' of an asset, and how is depreciation calculated?

If you were to buy a new car and sell it six months later, you would be unlikely to get the same price as you paid for it because its value will have fallen, or 'depreciated'.

The same applies to the assets a company uses in its business. The amount of use a company gets out of those assets during the year is charged as a cost to the Profit and Loss Account. It hasn't actually cost anything in cash terms once the asset has been purchased, but it is a way of apportioning the cost of an asset over its estimated useful life.

The estimated useful life of an asset can vary from, for example, four years for a car to fifty years for a building which is held on a fifty year lease. Occasionally, an asset such as a lease may be revalued in the accounts if its worth is much greater than that stated in the accounts. In this instance the depreciation charge will be calculated so as to write off the revised value over the remaining years of the lease.

Thus, if a company spends £1,000 on a crushing plant which should last for five years before becoming valueless, each year the Profit and Loss Account will be charged with the 'usage' of that plant, eg $£1,000 \div \frac{1}{5} = £200$

The are two main methods of calculating depreciation:
1 'Straight line' depreciation, as in the above example, by which an equal annual charge is made over the asset's estimated useful life.
2 'Reducing balance', by which a percentage of the asset's written down value at the end of the previous year (that is, the value after charging that year's depreciation) is charged in the current year.

There is a less common method called 'the sum of the digits' which charges greater depreciation in the early years of an asset's life.

Q

I have heard a lot about 'historic' cost and 'current' cost in the preparation of accounts. What do the terms mean?

Accounts have traditionally been prepared under what is called the 'historic cost convention'. This means that the company's assets and liabilities are recorded in the accounts at the amounts they cost when purchased or taken on. Similarly, the depreciation, or usage, of an asset was charged to the Profit and Loss Account based on that original cost.

However, many people argue that in times of inflation it is misleading to compute a depreciation figure at the same rate over a number of years. Accounting for inflation is the essence of current cost accounting. While the idea itself is a sound one, its implementation is fraught with problems, mainly because estimating the 'current' value of different kinds of assets in different industries involves too many subjective decisions.

Today, while some companies use current cost accounts, most have retained the historic convention, occasionally modified by the revaluation of certain assets, principally land and buildings.

Q

Our business is profitable but our auditors have warned us to keep an eye on working capital. Why is this so important?

Companies which appear to be trading profitably may collapse because they run out of cash. The health of a business depends on the availability of short-term funds that enable it to perform its normal trading operations. Usually defined as the difference between current assets and current liabilities, these funds are known as working capital.

Part of this working capital is 'locked-up' in stocks and debtors. If too much is tied up in these two items, you may not have enough cash to pay your creditors.

In order to avoid a cash flow crisis, your company should carefully monitor each item of working capital:
● Raw materials, stocks and stores – aim to receive supplies just before they are required, rather than have money tied up in materials which will not be needed for some time.
● Finished goods – aim to move finished goods to customers as quickly as possible, so you can invoice them instantly.
● Debtors – credit sales are virtually unavoidable, unless you're involved in retailing, where most sales are for cash. Try to achieve a balance between giving good credit terms and operating a strict debt collection policy. Also, make sure that your paperwork is despatched promptly.
● Creditors – make every effort to use suppliers who allow a generous credit period before requiring payment, as long as their prices don't reflect this privilege. Use your creditors effectively to fund as large a part of your stock and debtors as possible.

Don't, however, become overzealous in your pursuit of working capital efficiencies. If, for example, you go too far in extracting credit from your suppliers, you'll waste time in holding them off, and you may find your discount removed or your supplies cut. Business is a two-way operation, and it pays to be reasonable.

Q

We are a small company and we make a reasonable profit. We wish to expand, but first we have to raise capital to finance the growth. What preparatory work should be done?

You need to prepare a business plan, outlining the potential growth in sales and the expenditure necessary to achieve it. Some elements in the plan will be:
● A history of the company and an outline of its business operations.
● Market conditions.
● The company's expansion plans.
● A cash flow forecast.
● Past accounts.
● Details of the company's key personnel.

Begin by deciding on the rate, the timing and the direction of the expansion you hope to achieve. Then produce the cash flow forecast to support your plan. Remember not to be too optimistic because you will have to defend your proposal against tough questioning (even if you don't, be prepared).

The forecast you produce should indicate the type of funding you require – that is, long- or short-term, loan or equity, or a combination of alternatives. Show an awareness of potential risks by giving 'worst-case' and 'best-case' outcomes.

Q

We're facing a cash flow crisis, but our bank won't help. What should we do?

Is the crisis temporary or likely to be permanent? Depending on the circumstances, you have several options:
1 If you own the freehold of your property, consider a sale-and-leaseback arrangement. This means selling land or a building to, say, an insurance company or a pension fund, which then leases it back to you for a fixed term. This way, the seller gets the capital value while retaining use of the asset.
2 Dispose of any assets which are under-used or peripheral to your main activities.
3 Dispose of part of your business – for example a product line that no longer fits the overall marketing strategy. Ensure that it's an autonomous unit whose sale won't lead to the business's disintegration.
4 Sell an asset which fails to make a reasonable percentage return on the capital invested in it.
5 Try to raise equity capital from new business partners.
6 If you are owed money by customers, you may obtain a percentage of it at once by assigning your debtors to a 'factor', who will himself collect the full amount.

Q

We have won a big order to supply electronic components to a valued and reliable customer. How can I be sure we can afford to take it on?

1 Prepare a simple cash flow forecast (*see opposite page*), showing your cash inflows and outflows over the contract period. Check the figures carefully and anticipate shortfalls well in advance – a shortage of cash three months into production could put an end to the project.
2 Arrange with your customer to give you stage payments.

Alternatively, take your forecast to the bank and arrange a loan to cover any temporary short-fall, giving yourself room to manoeuvre.
3 Keep a sharp lookout for other problem areas of cash flow:
● Rising costs.
● A rise in interest rates.
● Late delivery of raw materials, or production delays due to industrial action, which could delay stage payments.
● Customer's postponement of delivery date, leading to loss of revenue.
● Customer's late payment.

Company reports **128–9** *Profit and growth* **156–7**

Q

How accurate are cash flow forecasts?

As with any forecast, they are only as accurate as the assumptions (about sales targets, cost levels, debtor collection periods, for example) upon which they are based. You must, therefore, give thought to their preparation and be realistic about timing. A large sale today may not turn into cash for one or two months.

Planning your cash flow will help you decide when, for instance, you can afford to splash out on a new piece of machinery or a bonus payment to your staff.

Q

We need to supplement our cash flow occasionally to cover periods between receipts for large orders. What options are open to us?

These temporary dips into the red are best met by arranging a simple overdraft facility with your bank manager, by arranging for more trade credit from suppliers or by setting up invoice discounting.

If they recur, it may mean the company is undercapitalized and more permanent funding will be required, from a rights issue or business institution, for instance.

Q

In our company, sales on credit are really unavoidable, but debtors delay until the last moment before paying their bills. How can we cut down on large outstanding amounts?

Do you get good credit references before supplying new customers? Make your terms more attractive by offering discounts for prompt payment.

In extreme cases, you may have to resort to legal proceedings. Consider bringing in a credit control specialist to advise you.

CASH FLOW FORECAST: 1988

£000

	JAN	FEB	MAR	APR	MAY	JUN	1ST HALF TOTAL
INFLOW (revenue)							
Cash Sales	100	100	150	200	250	250	1050
Credit Sales	200	225	250	300	300	375	1650
Sundry Income	–	–	20	–	–	30	50
	300	325	420	500	550	655	2750
OUTFLOW (costs)							
Production	150	150	175	200	200	200	1075
Sales	75	75	80	100	100	120	550
Marketing	75	75	50	80	80	65	425
Administration	50	50	65	60	60	80	365
Capital	–	–	–	–	40	–	40
Taxation	–	–	–	75	–	–	75
	350	350	370	515	480	465	2530
BALANCE BROUGHT FORWARD	50	0	(25)	25	10	80	50
NET INFLOW (OUTFLOW)	(50)	(25)	50	(15)	70	190	220
BALANCE CARRIED FORWARD	0	(25)	25	10	80	270	270

Financial modelling **150–1** *Equity and ownership* **154–5**

Q

The accountant has introduced standard costing as a measurement of performance. How does it work in practice?

'Standard costs' are directly related to budgetary control. They are predetermined estimates of the cost of performing a certain operation within a normal set of working conditions.

Provided the costs are properly prepared, the system is an invaluable guide to the performance of a production process.

The costs are based on a budgeted output and should be realistic and attainable. They provide a measure by which cost variances can be identified and controlled at the point they are incurred.

These variances – whether adverse or favourable – are then divided into one of three categories; depending on what has caused them:
1 Changes in the price of materials or the cost of labour and overheads used in a process.
2 The efficiency of labour and materials usage in achieving a certain output from a given set of inputs.
3 Changes in the volume or activity (capacity) of the business and the ability to recover overhead costs.

Q

I know that process costing is used mostly in manufacturing for working out the unit cost of a product. How is it calculated?

Each 'cost element' of a larger process is treated separately in process costing. A cost-per-unit figure is calculated for each element by dividing the total cost over a certain period by the number of units produced.

These cost elements – which include both direct and indirect costs – are then added together to give the total cost of the process.

As in any continuous operation, there are incomplete units, known as work-in-progress. These are costed as 'effective' units. For example, 200 half-completed units would be represented by 100 effective units. Average costs are used to value complete units transferred to the next process and work-in-progress.

The major difficulty with process costing is the problem of allocating joint costs to individual operations.

Q

I have a good idea for a product which I think will fit in well with our existing range. I want to do some research on costing to make sure it is feasible before I present it to my superiors. Where should I start?

You should examine the main areas of costing in turn:
1 Find out whether additional fixed costs (such things as rent, office and administration expenses, additional capital equipment) will be incurred in setting up production, or whether there is surplus capacity which could be used.
2 Calculate the direct costs associated with the product.
3 Determine the break-even figure – that is, how much you need to produce and sell in order to cover your additional fixed costs. Beyond that, further sales are clear profit once their marginal cost has been covered.

Thereafter, it is up to the sales and marketing people to decide whether they could meet your minimum targets, having taken into account their additional sales and marketing costs.

Q

What does our financial accountant mean when he talks about marginal costs?

Marginal cost means the extra cost incurred through increasing production by one unit. It is the variable cost of the production of that unit – in materials, labour and overheads.

The difference between marginal cost and selling price represents the contribution to fixed costs and profits made by that product. Once all fixed costs have been covered, you've reached the break-even point, and all contributions after that point are profit.

Because marginal costing avoids the problems associated with the absorption of fixed overheads into units of production, cost decisions can be based on a true cost-profit-volume relationship.

Q

Overheads in our section are getting out of hand. It's my responsibility to look after costs and keep them within acceptable limits. How can I make savings?

Use your initiative to attack the problem directly. A company which occupied the whole of a large building found its business was shrinking but not its overheads. So it moved into the top two floors and let out the rest of the space at competitive rates. In this way it saved on overheads and could expand again when profits improved.

Consider the following tactics, but always bear in mind the knock-on effect of change in other sections of the company, particularly industrial relations/Personnel:

● Switching from employing full-time to freelance staff.

● Reducing floor space, to cut outgoings in rent and rates.

● Examining the efficiency of all working practices: are they taking up too much space or using too much energy?

● If the work is cyclical, could you manage by employing temporary staff for short periods?

● Sub-contracting work. Significant savings could be made by placing work with outsiders who have specialist equipment and expertise instead of replacing worn-out machines.

● The introduction of new technology, but remember you're unlikely to make savings in the short term.

The way production costs are overtaken by sales is shown on the graph. When production is at 40% capacity, total costs will be £60,000, but sales revenue only £38,000. When production is at 100% capacity, sales reach £92,000 and total costs only £83,000. When the company's production is 83%, costs and revenue meet at £75,000 – the break-even point.

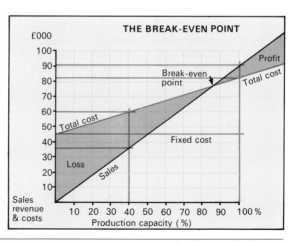

THE BREAK-EVEN POINT

Q

I dislike preparing budgets for projects because they take up so much of my precious time. I'd prefer the MD to work out what I can spend. Why does he insist that project managers prepare their own budgets?

If the MD prepared budgets for your projects, you'd have to provide the information and let the MD assess what you need to spend to make the project work. It makes much more sense for you, the budget holder, the manager responsible for the spending, to work out what you need.

If budgets were imposed from above you'd find they would tend to constrain rather than motivate you.

Budgets take time to construct and monitor, but they are well worth the effort.

They help you by:
● Forcing you to think ahead and plan for the future.
● Providing a check on expenditure as well as realistic targets.
● Enabling you to take immediate action on early warning signs (cash deficiencies, production bottlenecks, need for increased investment, and so on).

Q

Sometimes I have difficulty in getting the departmental supervisors to give me projections on which to base the budget. I think they are unwilling to be pinned down in case their estimates are way out. Is consultation really important?

It should be the vital element of your budget. Successful budgets aim to be as realistic as possible. You need those supervisors to give you their judgment, based on experience. So it's important for you to pin them down.

Some of the benefits of consultation are:
● Increased motivation.
● More realistic goals.
● Involvement from the start which makes it easier to change things later if they don't work out.

Remember that your supervisors are the people who are going to have to turn your budget into action. It is, therefore, in both your interests to agree the figures; otherwise you may end up with an unrealistic and unworkable budget.

Q

I have to prepare a departmental budget. Where do I begin?

Your starting point is the 'limiting factor'. In some companies, forecast demand is the factor: the sales budget is drawn up first, based on a market forecast of 'How many can we sell?'

In other companies the limiting factor may be the availability of capital: they may have to plan within strict financial bounds.

When preparing a budget, each department assesses its individual costs, once the sales department has decided how many items it thinks can be sold.

Labour, raw materials and overhead costs together constitute 'production costs'. To these are added operating expenses. The itemized capital-to-be-spent is matched with the income accruing from sales revenue and other items presented in the detailed cash flow.

Manufacturing companies may be constrained by their production facilities: they start with the question, 'How many can we make?'

Subsidiary budgets have to be balanced so as to adjust to targets for limiting factors imposed by one department on another.

Once you have decided on your department's major limiting factor, or have been informed of the parameters within which you must operate, assess all the costs associated with this level of commitment. Then:

● Compare your budget with the overall budget guidelines and make sure your objectives are consistent, and the results compatible with them.

● Set your budget parameters so that the target is neither too easy to achieve, nor too difficult.

● Assign responsibility for achieving each section of the budget.

● Allow for negotiation – budgets are rarely agreed as they stand.

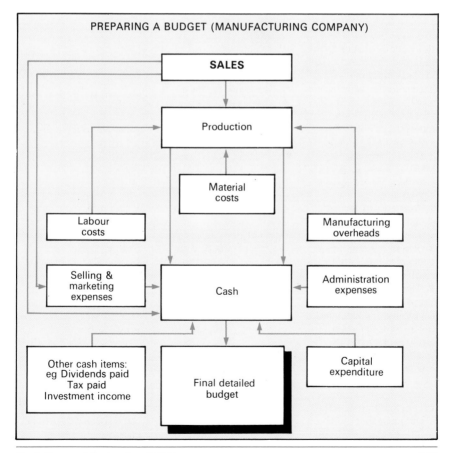

PREPARING A BUDGET (MANUFACTURING COMPANY)

SALES

Production

Material costs

Labour costs

Manufacturing overheads

Selling & marketing expenses

Cash

Administration expenses

Other cash items: eg Dividends paid Tax paid Investment income

Final detailed budget

Capital expenditure

Q

I'm responsible for my company's sales budget. How do I check that we are on target?

Keeping a close eye on a budget requires clear strategy, firm objectives, strict monitoring, fast corrective action and a willingness to learn.

A budget figure is a notional figure based on likely costs and/or likely sales. The real and budgeted figures will always differ. So the control of 'variances' is vital.

You must determine how soon you need to know of any variance in budgeted figures so as to do something about it. Base your calculations on 'worst case' forward planning, with the maximum allowance for any eventuality.

The fundamental steps are to:

1 Establish corporate objectives.
2 Prepare a budget by examining individual cost centres.
3 Combine individual budgets and eliminate inconsistencies.
4 Have the final budget approved by board or senior body. Inform cost centre. (At this stage, production or trading commences.)
5 Compare performance with budgeted figures.
6 Investigate variances.
7 Take corrective action.
8 Use experience of the result in future planning.

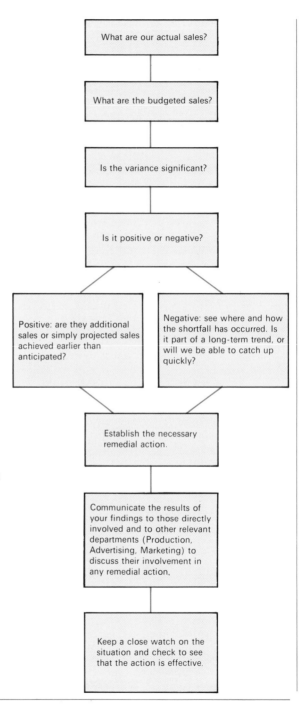

Q

For the last two years, my department has been spending well over budget. Head Office are blaming us for undermining their strategic objectives. What am I doing wrong?

You are adversely affecting the rest of the company. Your subsidiary budget must be playing havoc with the master budget at HQ.

Your department's budget is only a percentage of the company's overall profit objectives. It represents just one aspect of an agreed action plan.

You should have recognized the warning signs earlier but, equally, there should have been a feedback-and-review process that would have helped you get back on course. So:

● Carefully examine your budget now to see if you can find clues to the cause of overspending.

● Ensure that you are receiving information that is both timely and sufficiently detailed to form the basis of a proper review of departmental spending.

● Ask your management accountant to provide you with regular reports that highlight both favourable and unfavourable variances.

● Tighten up your control procedures, regularly reviewing actual results against the budget and following up the unfavourable variances.

● In future, make sure your budget is realistic. When you draw one up, you commit yourself to a plan for the future.

Once you can measure actual expense against your budget, you'll be in a position to take corrective action.

The people at HQ, however, must take some of the blame. It should be their job to ensure that all subsidiary budgets are:

● Realistically constructed.

● Committed to an agreed action plan.

● Coordinated to produce an overall picture of the company's objectives.

● Controlled to measure actual, against projected, performance.

● Used to take rapid remedial action.

Q

What is zero-based budgeting and how does it differ from flexible budgeting?

Zero-based budgeting, developed by Texas Instruments in the late 1960s, can be a useful way of preparing a budget by taking a step back and looking at the basic elements of a business.

It starts with the minimum level of activity required to maintain an acceptable operating level. (In effect, it assumes that you're starting from scratch, with each cost element justified separately.)

Separate 'decision packages' are then developed for levels above this, to show how funds would be utilized if available.

Funds can then be allocated according to whichever of these decision packages best satisfies the overall corporate objectives.

A flexible budget, on the other hand, starts with a normal level of activity. Within this level, costs are separated into fixed and variable, and the extent to which the variable costs will change within this normal range of activity is then determined. The budget is designed to change (to 'flex') depending on the level of activity actually achieved.

Q

What is computerized 'modelling' and should I use it?

Financial modelling is a technique whereby business plans are analyzed with the aid of a computer. A model is a representation of a specific situation or series of coordinates.

Before the advent of computers, the main constraint on modelling was the amount of time taken to build and calculate a model by hand – plus the difficulty of making changes and the problem of unnoticed calculation errors.

The micro-computer has solved these problems. You can use it to build models, change the parameters and recalculate results (projected well into the future) almost instantaneously.

Generally, a model of, say, a sales budget will be calculated for three scenarios – best, worst and 'most likely'. It is, in fact, unlikely that any of these will translate into reality.

A truer representation of the situation being modelled is given in advanced modelling packages. These use distributions of values for different variables, and take a random sample from these distributions to give a complete picture, which can be further analyzed using statistical techniques.

The elements of any model are the same; it's only the details that vary. A model comprises data for the variables that are to be assessed and the logic that links them.

Once the logical framework has been constructed, the data can be entered, calculations carried out and the results analyzed. But a model is only as good as the information put into it, and the results obtained are only guides as to what might happen.

Q

My department head has asked me to investigate whether we should replace one of our production processes, which is particularly labour-intensive and in need of renewal, with a highly automated process. He has given us some information on the equipment we would need, together with our potential sales figures for the next five years. Where do I start?

You must build a model of the production level necessary to satisfy anticipated sales. One part of the model should show what would happen if you retained the current production methods, the other should show the figures for the proposed automated method.

Ideally any model should be built on a computer, for flexibility and speed of calculation. But it involves no more than setting down all the relevant information on a spreadsheet (*see opposite*).

PRODUCTION DEPARTMENT – PROPOSED AUTOMATION

	Base costs/ needs	1987	1988	1989	1990	1991
PROJECTED UNIT SALES		25	30	35	45	50
Annual cost of inflation	5%					
MANUAL METHOD						
Manhrs/unit	2,000					
Total manhrs needed/annum		50,000	60,000	70,000	90,000	100,000
Standard hrs/workstation manhrs/year	10,000					
Capital cost/workstation ($)	25,000	25,000	26,250	27,562	28,941	30,388
Annual overhead cost/ workstation ($)	2,500	2,500	2,625	2,756	2,894	3,039
Labour cost/manhr ($)	6.00	6.00	6.30	6.61	6.95	7.29
No. of workstations needed		5	6	7	9	10
No. of new workstations needed		5	1	1	2	1
Capital costs of new workstations ($)		125,000	26,250	27,562	57,881	30,388
Total annual overhead costs ($)		12,500	15,750	19,294	26,047	30,388
Total annual labour costs ($)		300,000	378,000	463,050	625,117	729,304
TOTAL ANNUAL COSTS ($)		**437,500**	**420,000**	**509,906**	**709,045**	**790,080**

	Base costs/ needs	1987	1988	1989	1990	1991
AUTOMATED METHOD						
Machine hrs/unit	500					
Total machine hrs/annum		12,500	15,000	17,500	22,500	25,000
Operational hrs/machine	6,500					
Manhrs/machine	6,500					
Capital cost/machine ($)	250,000	250,000	262,500	275,625	289,406	303,877
Overhead cost/machine ($)	12,500	12,500	13,125	13,781	14,470	15,194
Labour cost/manhr ($)	6.00	6.00	6.30	6.61	6.95	7.29
No. of machines needed		2	3	3	4	4
No. of new machines needed		2	1	0	1	0
Capital costs of new machines ($)		500,000	262,500	0	289,406	0
Total annual overhead costs ($)		25,000	39,375	41,344	57,881	60,775
Total annual labour costs ($)		75,000	94,500	115,762	156,279	182,326
TOTAL ANNUAL COSTS ($)		**600,000**	**396,375**	**157,106**	**503,566**	**243,101**

DCF FOR MANUAL METHOD AT 12%	1,987,311
DCF FOR AUTOMATED METHOD AT 12%	1,421,495

Q

Why are companies valued, and how is the worth of a business calculated?

Companies are valued before any major change such as:

● When a takeover bid is imminent.
● If the business is to be merged with another.
● For flotation on the Stock Market.
● For assessing capital taxes.

Its value can be assessed in two ways:

1 By the asset basis – that is, the value of the assets used by the company (both fixed and current), less its current and long-term liabilities. The resulting figure represents shareholders' funds; dividing it by the number of shares gives a value per share.

● The methods used to value the assets will normally be those used to produce the company's accounts, except that assets such as freehold land will be valued according to the market values. This method values the business on a 'going concern' basis.

● Alternatively, the assets may be valued on a 'break-up' basis, showing the price they'd fetch if they were sold off separately, rather than as part of an active trading concern. This will often produce a significantly lower figure than the 'going concern' basis.

● A third method is valuation on

'replacement cost', that is, the cost of setting up a similar business from scratch.

2 On the earnings basis – this method is based on a company's earnings after all charges have been met but before a dividend is paid out to shareholders. Dividing this figure by the number of shares in an issue gives the earnings-per-share figure.

This figure is used in the price-earnings ratio, calculated by dividing the company's market price by its earnings figure. To value a company, you take an average of the price-earnings ratios for similar companies and apply that ratio to the earnings-per-share figure, in order to calculate a price per share.

The ratio depends, however, on estimates of future profitability, so it may be misleading to use last year's profit figures.

The earnings basis is considered the more subjective valuation method because it tries to assess future profitability.

When using the assets basis, a figure will be added for 'goodwill', in recognition of the fact that a trading company is more than just a collection of assets.

Q

I often look up my company's share price in the newspaper to see if it is going up or down. How is the price arrived at and why does it change?

The price of a share is calculated in the same way as the value of the business as a whole, since a share is genuinely a share of the business. It depends on how outsiders see your company and what they are prepared to pay for a 'piece of the action'.

If your company is growing rapidly, stockbrokers and other analysts who recommend purchase or sale of shares will try to estimate its future profit potential. Thus, if there is a sudden, unexplained drop in profits or if a planned new product has to be scrapped, the share price is likely to fall sharply.

Sometimes, companies are examined on the basis of what their assets would realize, if the business were to be broken up or on what the company might be worth to a potential bidder wishing to expand in that area.

Share prices are also affected by hearsay. A share may be 'talked up' on rumours of, for instance, a takeover bid, only to collapse when nothing of any substance emerges.

Q

What is gearing, and how does it affect the value of a business?

Gearing is the relationship between shareholders' funds (owners' capital) and long-term debt (loan capital) expressed as a percentage or a ratio. So a company with shareholders' funds of £20m and borrowing of £5m will have a gearing ratio of 1:4. Borrowings may be calculated as including bank overdrafts if they are a permanent source of a company's finance.

Income gearing is a complementary calculation and shows the relationship of profit to interest paid on borrowings. If profits are £100,000 and interest payment £75,000, 75%, this percentage shows that the company is vulnerable to a rise in interest rates.

A highly-geared company (where loan capital is high in proportion to equity) is a riskier, less stable venture. If the company has a year of low profit, it may not be able to meet the interest payments on its loans.

Investors are generally wary of any highly geared companies, but at times the high level of gearing will only be temporary. For example, a company may incur additional borrowings to finance the takeover of another company, but it will aim to reduce these borrowings by disposing of some of the assets or divisions of the target company when it gains control.

A low gearing ratio means a company has little interest-bearing capital compared with ordinary shares and is more likely to withstand adverse changes in the economic climate.

Managements may increase the gearing by raising further interest-bearing funds which can be used to earn a greater return than the interest charge. This, in turn, means greater profits for ordinary shareholders.

There is no one 'right' approach to gearing: used well, it can substantially enhance the value of a business, but used unwisely it can destroy it.

Q

My small clothing business is quite profitable, and I now wish to buy another company dealing in footwear. What should I look out for?

You should consider two main areas:
1 How the business will complement your existing activities.
● Would the acquisition improve profit margins?
● Could you use a single sales force for both types of product?
● Could you increase the market share for both products by selling a complete package of goods?
2 The potential of the business for sale. Ideally, look for a company whose owners and managers would be susceptible to your approaches. Ask yourself why the owners are disposing of the business.
● Do they want to realize their investment?
● Does the company have problems that need an injection of capital or expertise?
● Do they need to meet a cash flow crisis by a quick sale?

Cash flow and forecasting **142–3** *Equity and ownership* **154–5**

Q

Our company is small but we have enormous growth potential. Where can we raise the finance to expand?

The main sources of finance open to you are:

1 Venture capital. Pension funds, investment trusts, and other financial institutions are often interested in companies with growth potential that need money to expand.

The body providing the capital will generally want part of the company's equity, or share capital. They may put up the balance of the money required as a loan. Repayment of loans is usually tied to cash flow so that the company always retains adequate working capital.

Some investors like to get involved in 'hands-on' management. Others may be content with a more passive role and a supervisory seat on the board.

2 The Unlisted Securities Market. In the UK, the USM allows companies to raise money from investors, without having to face the more stringent requirements of a full listing on the Stock Exchange. This 'second tier' market also exists in many other countries.

The company's capital base expands with new investors, but the owners generally retain management and voting control. A minimum of 10 per cent of the equity must be in public hands.

3 A full listing on the Stock Exchange. This option is available only to relatively large companies, since it is an expensive process. At least 25 per cent of the equity must be in public hands.

At first, the Stock Exchange provides only a market place in which to buy and sell existing shares in the company. But once it has gained a reputation, the company will be able to increase its equity base by issuing fresh shares.

4 In addition, you may be able to raise money from private investors. Tax concessions granted by governments, such as the UK's Business Expansion Scheme, encourage investment in new or small businesses.

Q

I don't want to give up any equity in my company. Is it possible to fund the business through long-term loans?

For a sound business, longer-term finance can be made available for any period, usually for at least three years. It depends on how long the lender wants to tie up his/her money and on what he/she thinks of the prospects for your company. You may have to give an equity sweetener of a small amount, say 5 per cent.

A common method of long-term lending is by issue of loan stock, on which interest is payable at a rate usually linked to a particular bank's base rate. The loan stock can be of two types:

1 Straightforward repayment, with the capital sum due at the stock's redemption date.

2 The option of repayment or conversion into the company's ordinary shares.

Loan stocks are usually secured by a charge on the company's assets. So if a company is wound up, the holders of the stock rank for payment before the ordinary creditors. The charge can be either fixed (secured on a particular asset) or floating (secured on all the assets). A fixed charge ranks before a floating charge.

Q

How does a company get on to the Stock Exchange and who decides its market price?

A company must first satisfy the various Stock Exchange rules. A prospectus will then be prepared in conjunction with the company's advisers and a decision made as to how many shares it wants to release to the public and at what price. The price may be fixed or it may be a tender offer, with a minimum guide price, so that investors can decide how much they are prepared to pay.

If the shares are to be offered to the public at large, an 'offer for sale' will be made. Alternatively, the company's shares may be 'placed' with institutions or a stockbroker's other clients, who agree in advance the number of shares they will take at an agreed price.

Generally, offers for sale are 'underwritten', that is, several institutions will agree to take up any shares not applied for in the public offer for sale, in return for a fee.

Q

Our company has just been taken over by a conglomerate. What actually happens in a takeover or merger, and what are the benefits?

If the conglomerate has gained control of your company by acquiring its share capital from the existing owner, then a takeover has occurred.

Generally speaking, if the terms being offered by the prospective buyer are accepted by more than 50 per cent of the shareholders, control has been achieved. The remaining shareholders will accept the terms offered, although they are not obliged to do so.

If the shares are listed on the Stock Exchange, there are strict rules as to the percentage of shares of a target company a bidder can purchase, and the period within which he can do so.

In contrast, a merger joins the two companies in a 'marriage', whereby the assets of each company are merged into one. Shareholders of one or both companies exchange their shares for shares in the other.

The benefits of a takeover or merger vary according to whether or not both companies produce the same product or service. If they do, the advantages are:

● Economies of scale, especially in such areas as Personnel, advertising, marketing, accounting and distribution.

● Access to new markets.

● Better use of financial resources.

If the companies are in different fields, there are several benefits in diversification:

● The employment of under-utilized capital or managerial resources.

● Simply by becoming larger, a company may ward off an unwanted takeover.

●. A company's survival may depend on its getting out of a dying industry and into a new rapidly expanding growth area, in other words, there is diversification of risk.

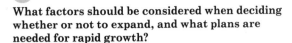

Q

What factors should be considered when deciding whether or not to expand, and what plans are needed for rapid growth?

You must examine:

● The market, and your company's place in it. Is it really a growth area?

● The competition, and what they are likely to do.

● Technological change. Are there advances which you will have to prepare for?

● New markets. Are there other areas for expansion which are complementary to your own? Remember to make a realistic assessment of your ability to enter a new market, particularly if you do not have a great deal of expertise in that area.

● Type of growth. Should you go for organic growth, or would it be more sensible to go for a takeover or merger with another company? You might also consider joint ventures.

● External factors (which are often outside your control): the political and economic climate; overseas competition.

For rapid growth, you need to plan realistically on several fronts:

1 Produce a detailed and comprehensive financial plan which examines the best and worst possible outcomes of expansion.

2 Assess the impact of expansion on your core business, to make sure it doesn't get neglected.

3 Ask yourself if the company's current administration is flexible enough to accommodate growth.

4 Be aware of the dangers of trying to sell too much.

5 Think ahead about the sources of capital for expansion – not just for immediate costs, but to fund a new factory or service facility.

6 Employees. Can you promote existing staff to fill new jobs, or must you recruit outsiders? Explain as much as possible to your staff, so they feel involved in the company's new enterprise.

Q

Our company is growing fast these days, but I'm afraid our sales manager, who's been with us from the start, is getting completely out of his depth. What should I do about him?

It's an old problem; headlong expansion always leaves some people behind, unable to keep up with new demands. It's no help to a company to have an employee struggling to fill a key role.

Business is business, so it's vital that you have the right person for the job. But that doesn't mean you should get rid of your sales manager. If his skills and knowledge are valuable to the company, consider moving him over to train your sales staff.

Q

Our position in the market has now been consolidated and we're thinking of going public to finance future growth. What are the problems in such a move?

There are several potential problems:
● Timing – is the economic climate favourable? Is the company ready for it?
● Taxation – how will going public affect the personal tax position of the current owners?
● Finance – controls must be tight, and the finance department must be able to cope with increased reporting requirements. You will have to give the outside world a lot more information than you used to.
● The company will become more vulnerable to takeover through raids on shares.
● Shareholders – future policy decisions will have to take their interests into consideration.
● Senior management will have to spend a lot of time preparing for flotation, and a lot of time afterwards dealing with the Stock Exchange.
● There may, in future, be a temptation to take important decisions or significant action with too great an emphasis paid to the effect such decisions will have on the share price.

Q

We're a small company about to expand. I'm worried that our cosy working atmosphere will disappear. How can I make sure it does not?

In order to grow, there must be some changes, not all of them for the worse. If you want to maintain the cosy atmosphere, try setting up small autonomous units, responsible for their own budgets and work schedules within the company framework.

But why assume a larger company can't be a big happy family? Everyone feels involved in a small company because they feel that their work directly influences its development. So just continue communicating your objectives and progress to your staff.

Increase their involvement through a share option scheme, for instance.

Q

What is 'market capitalization'?

Market capitalization is the current market value per share multiplied by the number of shares in issue.

The current market price of a company fluctuates according to a number of factors, such as whether the company has produced consistent profits and what investors think its future may be.

It will also be affected by factors outside its control, such as the state of the industry, the economy and the political climate.

Q

We're a small company, just starting, and we can't afford to pay the market rate for employees. How can we attract the kind of people we need to make the company a success?

The answer is to link the fortunes of the company to the personal fortunes of each employee. Advertise the job as carrying a profit-sharing scheme, whereby employees are encouraged to devote themselves to the success of the company in return for a share of the profits. Profit-sharing highlights the contribution made by all those working for the organization.

Explain the situation to potential employees at their interviews (at which stage they should be feeling enthusiastic and receptive). State that while you cannot yet pay them what you think they're worth, once the business becomes profitable – with their help – their earnings will rise exponentially. If you are prepared to part with some of your equity in the company, consider some form of share option scheme.

The combination of commitment, work incentive and potentially high earning power is a potent one.

Q

We pay our sales staff low wages plus commission. Is this a better incentive than a high salary?

Any system of payments must be evaluated in terms of the company's financial and personnel needs. Consider whether a change to a high salary without commission would:
● Improve cash flow.
● Increase profits.
● Reduce turnover of personnel and thus the cost of recruiting and training new staff.
● Promote company loyalty.
● Increase motivation.
● Reduce the drive of assertive and ambitious sales staff.

Q

As manager of a medium-sized mail order company, how do I choose fringe benefits that will attract competent people without costing the earth?

Your choice of benefits should be tied as closely as possible to your own products. As you are a mail order company, you are well placed to offer your goods to employees below normal retail price.

Some companies allow staff to buy slightly damaged goods, 'seconds', at considerable discounts.

Try to match the benefits to the employees, and offer what is most appropriate to their *amour propre*. The benefits offered by some companies include:
● Profit sharing.
● Share option schemes.
● Company car.
● Expense account.
● Private medical insurance.
● Season rail tickets.
● Free medical check-ups.
● Subsidized canteens.
● Luncheon vouchers.

Q

The union has been pressing for sabbatical leave for its members. Why should employees have extra paid leave, and what are the advantages to the firm?

Sabbaticals allow employees to broaden their experience, add to their qualifications or improve their skills. Regular paid sabbaticals, offered after every five years of service for a period of about four weeks, have several advantages. They:
● Provide a well-earned 'breathing space'.
● Encourage longer service among employees.
● Give employees the chance to travel.
● Increase job satisfaction by providing further training.

Unfortunately, things may not work out so well. It's quite possible that:
● Disaffected employees may use the extra time to work for the competition.
● Departments may be understaffed at times.
● Arranging cover for employees away on sabbatical will involve additional costs.

Rather than offer sabbaticals as glorified holidays, give your employees interesting alternatives to their current work. Give them unpaid leave for special projects, for instance for a job swap with an executive from another company.

Q

It's been drawn to my attention that some members of the art department are freelancing for other companies – among them our direct competitors. How can I stop this happening?

It's clearly far from ideal to have staff working in any capacity for the opposition. The only way to stop it happening is to sack the main culprit as an awful warning to others – provided, that is, his or her contract specifically precludes working for other companies 'involved in similar activities'.

But why do your staff need extra work? Aren't you paying them enough? Aren't you making enough demands on them? Are they lacking stimulation, challenge and recognition of their worth? It is your responsibility to make sure that your personnel are working to full capacity and that they are satisfied with their jobs.

Q

Our area sales manager travels a lot on company business, and has a company car. Now our company sales manager has asked for one, although he does comparatively little travelling. Must everyone have a car today?

What would happen if the area sales manager were promoted to company sales manager? You'd hardly take his car away from him . . .

The company car is hard to beat as a fringe benefit. Even if it isn't essential to a job, it's an important expression of executive status; even more so if the employee is allowed his choice of model. Paying the car's tax, insurance, servicing, repairs and petrol can all be thrown in as additional perks.

Q

Why do successful companies go in for franchising?

A franchise operation has many benefits:
● It allows an existing business to expand more rapidly than it could by using its own capital.

The first Body Shop, for example, was set up in Brighton in 1976 selling natural skin and hair care products. In less than ten years the first shop grew into a franchise chain of nearly 200 from Iceland to the Middle East.
● The cost of expansion is significantly less than it would be with a traditional branch network, as franchisees use their own funds to set up an outlet.
● The middle tiers of management are cut out, and the day-to-day staffing/administration problems are greatly reduced.
● It provides the franchisor with highly motivated managers who have a direct interest in maximizing profits; this in turn contributes to the franchisor's royalty income.
● As the company's reputation grows, opportunities for making favourable arrangements with suppliers grow apace.

Q

I'd like to be in control of a business but I don't want to take any risks. Is franchising the answer?

Taking on a franchise is a relatively safe way of making the transition from employee to entrepreneur. You have many of the advantages of belonging to a large organization, but you are your own boss on the premises, answerable only to your franchisor.

Is it important to realize at the outset what it means to work within the framework and constraints of the franchise system. The franchisor will not allow the business format to be changed and will retain the right to intervene. A formal contract drawn up by the franchisor's solicitors will lay down certain safeguards about the way the business is run and you will be given a detailed operating manual.

Otherwise there is wide scope for independent decision making. The following aspects will be entirely up to you:
● The hours of operation.
● The employment of staff and their wage levels.
● The book-keeping procedures.

Depending on the particular franchisor, you will also have some say in:
● The quality of customer service.
● Local advertising.

Since a franchise business usually deals with an identifiable, established product or service, decisions concerning the product itself are usually the franchisor's responsibility; these include additions or deletions to the product/service range and the pricing policy.

The franchisor will usually also control:
● The supply of goods.
● National advertising campaigns, for which the franchisee pays a levy.

The business risks are certainly minimized in a franchise operation, not least because the product/service involved is already a 'proven formula', with an established image and backed by advertising. Banks and investors can assess the operation at work before advancing you capital. The failure rate in franchising is very low.

In the UK, the British Franchise Association, a voluntary body set up to represent the interests of reputable franchisors, also helps franchisees to safeguard their interests.

I've been offered a job managing a shop under franchise. Does this arrangement mean that most of the profits will go to the franchisor?

In return for the right to sell a product with an established trade name, trade mark and business system, and the goodwill associated with it, the franchisee pays certain fees to the franchisor:

● A deposit – paid by a prospective franchisee to secure a particular location. This is often partly refundable if no agreement is ultimately reached.

● An initial franchise fee, which covers some of the costs (usually about 5–10 per cent) of setting up the franchise, such as training, shopfitting, research and development costs, legal and recruitment cost, and initial supplies.

● A weekly, monthly or annual franchise fee or royalty, based on a percentage of gross sales of the business; this is on average around 10 per cent and should never be more than 13 per cent of turnover.

Franchisors sometimes take their revenue as a mark-up on goods supplied, or by charging a fixed management service fee. But you should be wary if they propose taking their fee from more than one source.

● A contribution toward national advertising and promotion, which may be included in the royalty.

A percentage of the profits, is, therefore, paid to the franchisor, but there is still plenty of opportunity to build up a nice little equity for yourself in the business.

If the trade name is well known and you are prepared to work hard to get your outlet established, the profits should certainly be high enough to make franchising worthwhile.

I am thinking about becoming a franchisee for a fast food company. Once I've taken over the franchise, what support and continuing service can I expect?

The franchisor needs to maintain the high motivation of franchisees if the outlet is to be profitable.

There should, therefore, be a reliable system of support for the franchise outlet. The franchise contract itself should clarify the franchisor's intentions. You should be able to count on:

● Thorough initial training – most franchisees attend courses covering all aspects of the business.

● Professional back-up services – ranging from marketing to shopfitting.

● Specialist management services.

● Research and development, with updates of methods and innovations carried out at the franchisor's expense.

● Regular monitoring of your performance to maintain standards and profitability.

● Regular promotion and advertising campaigns.

● The financial benefits of bulk-buying.

INDEX

procedures,
organizational 20, 24
production levels 83
productivity bonuses 77
profitability 27, 131
Profit and Loss Account
128, 132–3, 140
consolidated 134–5
profits 131–6, 138, 156–7
attributable 134–5
company 153
franchising 160–1
gross 134–5
margins 27
operating 134–5
profit-sharing 158
project development 10
project management 28
project schedule 66–7
promotion 18–19, 24–5,
45–7, 50–1, 65, 70–2, 79,
82, 90
assessment 72
cultivating skills 43,
70–1
public relations 119, 129
public speaking 118–19
punctuality 32–3

Q
quality control system 27

R
Race Relations Board 54
ratio analysis 130–1
reading 45
receiver 89
recruitment, staff 26–7,
58–61, 74
redundancy 15, 81
references 48–9
staff 57
relaxation 15–19, 28, 97
relocation, job 18–19
office 101–2, 135
reports 25
company 128–9
reprimands 28, 80, 109
see also discipline
resources, departmental
83

responsibility, chain of
23, 80
revaluation reserve 132–3
rewards 77
rhythm, personal 37
risk 153
diversification of 155
role and position 85
routines, work 24, 28
rumours 109

S
sabbaticals 159
salaries 58, 76, 158–9
sales, cost of 134–5
scale, economies of 153,
155
scheduling 20, 29–30, 38,
78, 88
project work 66–7
secretary 30, 36, 52–3,
117, 123
security 56
self-awareness 10–11,
16–17, 20, 28, 42, 65,
84, 124
self-esteem 14
self-image 53
self-interest 77
shares, earnings
135–7
offer for sale 157
price of 152
types of 135
shares
value of 132–3
share capital, called up
132–3
shareholders 129, 132–3,
156–7
shareholding 155
share premium account
132–3
skills, developing 10–11,
42–5, 62, 108
intellectual 10
interpersonal 10
physical 10
technical 10
social life 14
social occasions 38, 124–5

social skills 124
software 105
Source and Application
of Funds, Statement of
128, 136–7
special projects 24
SSAF see Statement of
Source and Application
of Funds
staffing 26–7, 145, 158–9
stationery, conservation
of 34
status, executive 117, 159
stereotypes 61
Stewart, Rosemary 42
stock 136–7
valuation of 140
Stock Exchange listing
154
Stock Market 156–7
stress 12–19, 28, 54
assessing situations
14–15
coping with 12–15
decision making, effect
on 15, 32
exercise 14, 17
expressing emotions 14
problem solving, effect
on 15
travel and jetlag 16–17
see also relaxation
style, management 10–11,
45, 54–7, 64, 86–90, 117,
125
communication 122
success 42
supplies 130
systems 27

T
takeovers 25, 89, 155
talent 73
targets, budgetary 146–9
tasks, assignment 21, 68
taxation 134–5, 156
company 136–7
teams and groups,
managing 20–1, 35, 52,
57–8, 62–5, 68, 74, 76,
88–9, 93, 98

BIBLIOGRAPHY

Arthur Young (UK) *The Manager's Handbook* London, Sphere, 1986; New York, Crown, 1986

Armstrong, Michael *How to be a Better Manager* London, Kogan Page, 1983; New York, Nichols, 1984

Betts, Peter W. *Office Management* New York, David McKay, 1975; London, Hodder (paperback), 1986

Bowey, A. *Handbook of Salary and Wage Systems* Aldershot, Gower, 1982; Vermont, Gower, 1982

Brech, E.F.L. *Principles and Practice of Management* New York, Longman, 1976; London, Longman/Pitman (paperback), 1983

Dale, Ernest and Michelson, L.C. *Modern Management Methods* London, Pelican (paperback), 1969

Davis, William *The Corporate Infighter's Handbook* London, Sidgwick & Jackson, 1984; New York, Sidgwick & Jackson, 1985

Drucker, Peter F. *The Practice of Management* New York, Harper & Row, 1954; London, Heinemann, 1955, Pan (paperback), 1968

Drucker, Peter F. *The Effective Executive* New York, Harper & Row, 1967; London, Heinemann, 1967, Pan (paperback), 1970

Falk, Roger *The Business of Management* London, Pelican (paperback), 1978

Heller, Robert *Supermanagers* New York, E.P. Dutton, 1984; London, Sidgwick & Jackson, 1985

Iaconetti, Joan & O'Hara, Patrick *First-Time Manager* New York, Macmillan, 1985

Jay, Anthony *Management and Machiavelli* London, Hodder & Stoughton, 1967

Lee, T.A. *Company Financial Reporting* Philadelphia, International Ideas, 1976; Walton-on-Thames, Nelson, 1982, Wokingham, Van Nostrand Reinhold (paperback), 1985

McCormack, Mark H. *What They Don't Teach You at Harvard Business School* London, Collins, 1984, Fontana (paperback), 1986; New York, Bantam Books, 1985

Parker, Robert Henry *Understanding Company Financial Statements* London, Penguin (paperback), 1982

Parkinson, C. Northcote *Parkinson's Law* London, John Murray, 1958, Penguin (paperback), 1986; New York, Ballantine, 1986

Stewart, Rosemary *The Reality of Management* London, Pan (paperback), 1967, Heinemann, 1986

Taylor, William John & Wattling, Tom *The Basic Arts of Management* London, Business Books, 1972; Woodstock, N.Y., Beekman, 1972

Townsend, Robert *Up The Organization* New York, Alfred Knopf, 1970, Fawcett (paperback), 1978; London, Coronet (paperback), 1983

Turla, Peter & Hawkins, Kathleen L. *Time Management Made Easy* New York, E.P. Dutton, 1984; London, Panther (paperback), 1985

Vause, R. & Woodward, N. *Finance for Managers* London, Macmillan (paperback), 1981

Video Arts *So You Think You Can Manage?* London, Methuen, 1984

Publishers' acknowledgments

The publishers received invaluable help from the following people and organizations:

Donald Binney
Richard Hughes ACMA, MBA
Pat Hunter
Carole McGlyn
Candy Lee
Carolyn Sutherland
H. Beric Wright, MB, FRCS, MFOM
Stephen Bryant
Mike Titterton
Hayward & Martin
Space Planning Services Limited
Business Time/System
Time Manager International